"In *Playing in the Zone*, Andrew Cooper articulates perfectly why we are so captivated by sports. It's not just the excitement and beauty of athletic competitions that draws us but something deeper. Cooper shows, through sports, what is best in ourselves."

— JOAN RYAN, columnist at the *San Francisco Chronicle* and author of *Little Girls in Pretty Boxes: The Making and Breaking of Elite Gymnasts and Figure Skaters*

"More than any other book on the spiritual aspects of sport, *Playing in the Zone* puts it all together: science, myth, history, and the personal experiences of athletes of all stripes and levels. Beautifully written, with a critical eye and a keen wit, the book reveals what sports can mean to the inner life and why they can mean so much."

— DAVID MEGGYESY, former NFL linebacker, author of *Out of Their League*

"This book lifts sports into the realm usually reserved for art or religion, revealing the many ways in which it can both test and feed the human spirit. I am extremely grateful to Mr. Cooper for giving me a new appreciation for the great games and for those who play them."

— WES NISKER, news commentator at Pacifica Radio and author of *Crazy Wisdom*

"Superbly crafted and beautifully conceived, *Playing in the Zone* is fascinating, provocative, and a pleasure to read. The author demonstrates that, despite all that is wrong in our athletic culture, sports are at their heart a matter of deep and joyous spiritual significance."

— PAT TOOMAY, former Dallas Cowboy and Oakland Raider and author of *The Crunch*

"*Playing in the Zone* is that rarity: a work of real intellectual substance that is also a great read. Andrew Cooper has pulled this off with grace, humor, and originality. He challenges us to see past our cultural assumptions and into sport's deepest layers of meaning. But his approach is so personable that one feels altogether at ease with the material, as though he is simply articulating what one already knows."

— CARL E. PRINCE, Professor of History, New York University, author of *Brooklyn's Dodgers*

"Skillfully and eloquently, Andrew Cooper explores what it is about sports that allows them to exert so great a 'purchase on the soul.' In doing so, he shows how they can open to us a selfless awareness that expresses our deepest nature. This is a delightful, wise, and compelling book."

— TENSHIN REB ANDERSON, Roshi, senior dharma teacher, San Francisco Zen Center and author of *Warm Smiles from Cold Mountains*

personal attribute or possession. "In earliest Greece," says Singer, "a person could not be considered a hero until after death, when that heroic energy went into the society's store of ancestral blessings. Heroic energy was an impersonal force, what we would call archetypal. Today, we personalize heroism, which from the perspective of archetypal psychology is a big mistake."

By placing athletics in a mythological context—through ritual, through art, and through their general understanding of what athletics meant—the Greeks (and other ancient peoples) could connect with their games' archetypal content while maintaining the distinction between the athlete and the divine energy acting through the athlete's person. But today "we've collapsed the distinction between the person and the gods. We mistake the athlete for the divine element."

Archetypal experience holds great potential for both benefit and harm. An archetype cannot be said to be either morally good or evil; the effect it has depends on the quality of one's relationship to it. Singer believes that the activation of the numina in contemporary sport is often destructive in its consequences. In describing what is probably the most significant aspect of this, Singer refers to the *participation mystique*, a term Jung used often and which he borrowed from the French ethnographer Lucien Levy-Bruhl. Participation mystique is the forming of an unconscious identification with another person, a group, an object, or even an event. In the case of the sports fan, it means the loss of the ability to differentiate one's own life from the activity of a team or player or one's fellow fans. "It's a kind of inflation of the ego beyond its proper boundary. You get so puffed up that you cease to see an event for what it is. Lives get ruined because of it." Especially if your team is fumble prone.

Singer views our obsession with sports as symptomatic of a society in which individuals feel an absence of meaning. "When your life feels empty, there is an unconscious pull to project your deepest feelings onto mass events. One starts to live a collective life. The complexities of a truly lived individual life get projected on a team or player as a source of meaning. It is a kind of sickness, a sign that something is out of balance."

In activating the archetypal contents of the psyche, sport elicits feelings of the most profound sort. In *Baseball Fever* Singer writes on a serious note:

> For many people, their most passionate and deepest feelings are lived through their involvement with a player or team—a kind of ongoing active imagination through which all sorts of psychological phenomena are experienced. . . . Primitive, even atavistic, modes of perception, behavior, and thinking are activated in the fan's wish to see his (her) team win. . . . Levels of emotional experience normally forbidden in daily life find easy expression in the fan's unbridled hatred, sadism, gloating, ridiculing, and murderous rages.

Much of the madness and the joy of sport is attributable to its symbolic workings in the unconscious. This calls up a crucial question. What kind of relationship between the conscious and unconscious parts of the psyche would enhance the benefits of sport and minimize its destructiveness?

Mystery Plays

The question touches on the key concern of Jungian thought. A popular misconception has it that for Jung inner work promoted an identification of the ego with the archetypal forces. As Singer points out, this would be disastrous—the ego would simply be overwhelmed, its ability to perform its necessary functions undermined completely. The point is not to identify with the gods; quite the contrary, it is essential for the ego to differentiate itself from the archetypal energies, or it will be forced to live them out unconsciously.

But to speak only of differentiation can itself be misleading. In his autobiography, *Memories, Dreams, Reflections,* Jung writes that "the psyche is transformed and developed by the relationship of the ego to the contents of the unconscious." A conscious connection with the deeper layers of the psyche transforms and refines the raw archetypal energies and imbues consciousness with order, richness, and vitality.

For Jung, the goal of this process of inner transformation, the Self, was symbolized by the mandala, a type of image used in Buddhist and Hindu iconography. Generally, the basic design of a mandala is a circle that is symmetrically divided into four parts. Like the Self, a mandala is an integrated whole made up of differentiated parts. As the regulating center of the total psyche, the Self represents balance in the dynamic tension between the ego and the unconscious.

A type of dynamic tension is also at work in the second world of sport, that place where we step out of the everyday world to confront the archetypal forces. Indeed, the distinctiveness of the second world depends on it. According to Singer, without the tension between mana consciousness and rational consciousness, the reality of the second world collapses. The primal pull is great, but one can connect with the powerful energies sport unleashes without losing oneself in them. One can participate in the workings of potent symbols without literalizing them. In so doing, that borderline realm between jest and earnest—the home ground of both sport and myth—is maintained and nurtured.

The conscious mind is a player in this process, but it does not occupy center stage. This may be the single most compelling thing about witnessing a sporting event. Sport models the tensions and resolutions of psychic life from a perspective that includes, but does not revolve around, the ego. By weaving together the disparate, often contradictory strands of our nature into a coherent, harmonious whole, the second world of sport is a paradigmatic display of the Jungian Self.

In *Homo Ludens* Huizinga writes, "In the form and function of play, itself an independent entity which is senseless and irrational, man's consciousness that he is embedded in a sacred order of things finds its first, highest and holiest expression." For Huizinga play, by linking human consciousness with the "sacred order of things," constituted the foundation of human culture. Today science has replaced the traditional cosmologies with an indifferent universe, and social systems have been shown to be the creations of human beings rather than expressions of divine will or natural order. But psychologically, Huizinga's statement still works. A game has an inherent form, and in our playing out of that form we are, in turn, played by it. In sensing the form of a game, we recognize, however vaguely, that our individual consciousness exists in relation to a larger context. The ordering of events through the playing of a game models the ordering of the psyche through the "play" of its elements, a process mediated not by the ego but by the Self.

Despite the seemingly endless difficulties the modern West has encountered in its attempts to grasp the world of primal and ancient peoples, the sports we play today link us to that world, though they do so in ways we are not well equipped to recognize or understand. If we cannot fully grasp the experience of ancient peoples, we can, nonetheless, find points where it resonates with our own. If we cannot recreate the experience of athletics in the ancient world (and there is really no reason for us to try), we can locate elements of that experience in our own. This is, as Singer says, critical, because the inner meaning of sport rests on an ancient foundation, whose nature and significance is more available to imaginative recognition than to conceptual understanding. Nevertheless, attempts to clarify the ideas through which we frame the past, though always subject to refinement and critique, are necessary to bring these ideas into conformity with the historical record and thereby lend greater substance and accuracy to our intuitive perceptions.

In *Before Philosophy: The Intellectual Adventure of Ancient Man*, Henri Frankfort describes the predominant mode of consciousness among the ancients as *mythopoeic*, a term with much the same meaning as Singer's mana consciousness. But in unpacking the internal logic of mythopoeic thought, Frankfort avoids some of the European biases and "noble savage" romanticism that easily accrue to Jungian thought. According to Frankfort, mythopoeic thought is not a "pre-logical" mode of thinking. The people of the ancient world were quite capable of logical reasoning; it simply was not their preferred mode of religious thought: "For the detachment which a purely intellectual attitude implies is hardly compatible with their most significant experience of reality."

For ancient people, the world was "redundant with life." The phenomena of experience were encountered as living presences, with which one existed in a reciprocal relationship. This mode of experience required a means of expression inclusive of the whole person, the emotions and imagination as well as the intellect. The world was given coherence through the telling of stories—myths— that revealed life's paradigmatic forms. Myths served as models of life's essential activities and conditions. Ceremony, ritual, art, and sport expressed, deepened, and harmonized the interdependent connection between humans and the powers at work in the cosmos.

A world in which everything is alive, in which the cosmic life force, mana, pulses through all things, is a pretty far cry from what most of us experience nowadays. And yet the mode of consciousness by which that world is known is not so alien to us after all. Indeed, it is part of our makeup, and its allure is inescapable. We long to be touched deeply by the world, to experience the resonance of symbolic consciousness. For some, this need is met within the framework of depth psychotherapy or the broader culture of ideas it has spawned. On a larger scale, art and religion, now as always, can serve to call forth the deeper dimensions of our being. But for countless millions, the second world of sport is the most accessible and compelling theater for the quickening of mythic consciousness. Furthermore, for all the coarseness and chaos endemic to sports culture, we may still find in it some measure of instruction in negotiating the joys and dangers of symbolic experience.

During my last meeting with Tom, we meandered back to a

point he had raised in a previous conversation: the ancient belief that certain persons, objects, or events were particularly infused with mana. This, we agreed, is something one can feel with a compelling sense of reality in the world of sport. Certain athletes seem to be blessed with some intangible quality—an energy, almost a radiance—some hidden resource that gets called forth at a critical juncture.

Our conversation turns, almost inevitably, to Joe DiMaggio, for few figures in American sport have been so possessed of this something extra. Certainly this quality was recognized by Ernest Hemingway, who speaks of its reflective glow through the person of Santiago in *The Old Man and the Sea*: "I must have confidence and I must be worthy of the great DiMaggio who does all things perfectly even with the pain of the bone spur in his heel." In his thoughts, Santiago seems to invoke DiMaggio's presence, for DiMaggio embodies the courage, perseverance, and mastery that bring the favor of nature's unseen powers. The old man knows he will need these qualities of the great DiMaggio to endure in his great ordeal of bringing to shore the wondrous fish "which is my brother," for such fishes are "more able and more noble," more alive with the power of nature, than the fishermen who, like Santiago, must kill them. My father is seventy-five, and to this day, he, like the old fisherman, speaks with awe of DiMaggio as the epitome of natural grace. For millions of my father's generation—the generation that came of age during the Great Depression and World War II—DiMaggio's Olympian presence symbolized a kind of perfection that lent a measure of majesty to a strife-torn world.

As we speak, it is late October 1995, World Series time, and this year marks the Cleveland Indians' first appearance in the series since 1954. In their coverage, the sports media make frequent reference to a single play from that series forty-one years ago: Willie Mays's over-the-shoulder catch of Vic Wertz's mighty line drive. If ever a sports event glowed with the power of mana, it was that catch, and Mays's subsequent throw to the infield to hold the lead runner at third.

The 1954 Cleveland team had compiled the best regular-season record in modern Major League history, and they were heavily favored to beat Mays's New York Giants. In the first game of the series, with the score tied at two, Wertz crushed a Don Liddle pitch 460 feet into the depths of the Polo Grounds center field, the deepest in the game. At the crack of the bat, Mays took off, running full speed, his back to home plate. At the last moment, still at full stride, he bends his head back, extends his glove, and like a sparrow returning to its nest, the ball settles into Mays's grasp. Then, just as remarkably, Mays spins on a dime and makes a perfect 300-foot throw to prevent even one run from scoring. What should have been a triple, or even an inside-the-park home run, is now just another out.

The Giants went on to win the game and eventually the series in a four-to-zero sweep. Had it turned out differently, the play could well have broken the Giants' spirit. Instead, that was Cleveland's fate. And not only for the series. With that play, Cleveland began a plunge into a spiritless mediocrity that was to last for decades.

So now it is 1995, and in describing the Cleveland Indians' return to World Series play, sports commentators can scarcely avoid discussing the aura of magic that still surrounds the event. Mays's catch seemed to mark more than a shift in momentum; it seemed to occasion a shift of fate. That is what these mainstream sportscasters are talking about, and they are wondering whether things have finally shifted back in Cleveland's favor. They might as well be speaking of the favor of the gods, for as Michael Novak writes, fate is "the unseen god of sports events," presiding over sport as over life.

From one perspective this talk of fate is just an example of the necessary hyperbole of sports talk. If you were to ask, say, Bob Costas whether he believed that these events *really* represented the workings of fate or some supernatural agency, my guess is that he would say no. But whether or not one believes in such things, to those with faith in the game, fate *feels* like an actual presence.

The question of whether the transpersonal forces—fate, mana, God and gods, and so forth—are psychological projections or objective realities is a necessary question for the rational mind. But as Frankfort and others have pointed out, such questions, based as they are on a detached distance from experience, on a series of sharp dichotomies—subject and object, inside and outside, reality and appearance—such questions are foreign to the mythic mode of thought, in which either/or distinctions don't apply. Or rather, they apply solely on a practical level. Mythic thought reflects an experience of continuity among all aspects of a single reality.

Frankfort writes, "Whatever is capable of affecting mind, feeling, or will has thereby established its undaunted reality." In the second world of sport, we can feel the presence of transpersonal agencies without the burden of assigning to such feelings theological or scientific justification. In a world that is otherwise hostile to its viewpoint, the mythic mind finds in sport room to play. Does Earvin Johnson really possess some quality of magic? Was there really a mysterious force guiding the Celtics in the old Boston Garden? Did the great DiMaggio actually display not just grace but Grace? Reason may tell us one thing, but feeling says something else. The rational mind wants an answer. The mythic mind wants mystery.

In *Gods and Games: Towards a Theology of Play*, David Miller describes the nineteenth century's Romantic philosophers' recognition that feeling must be primary in human meaning if our experience is to have a sense of coherence, harmony, and significance. The Romantics argued that the West's long historical attempt to place rationality at the center of human meaning had led to a fragmented, isolated consciousness, in which the relatedness of God and humanity, humanity and nature, the sacred and the secular, feeling and thinking, and so forth had been severed by the dichotomous logic of rational thought.

For the Romantics, aesthetics served as a better basis for discerning meaning in human existence than did reason. They saw modeled in the creativity of art the means to a revitalized relationship to the world. Their perception of meaning as a creative process eventually led them to discover in play the active expression of the unified meaning they sought. For in play a context is created in which experience is characterized by freedom, order, coherence, beauty, and vitality.

In Miller's view, play, like religion, requires faith.

> Faith is being gripped by a story, by a vision, by a ritual (game). It is being seized, being gripped by a pattern of meaning, a pattern of meaning that affects one's life-pattern, that becomes a paradigm for the way one sees the world. . . . Faith is make-believe. It is playing as if it were true. It is not that the religious story is not true. It is simply that questions of truth are irrelevant while in the midst of make-believe, while in the midst of faith.

To play or watch a game is to live poetically. It is to participate, with faith, in a process of imagining a reality within which one thinks and acts. Games are not unique in this regard. To the contrary, they simply make evident something we do all the time. We humans are storytelling creatures, and we live our lives by means of the stories we tell ourselves. Whether in religion, science, art, politics, or any other field, we give order and meaning to our lives by fashioning stories from events.

According to Miller, we apprehend the world by means of *poiesis* (creativity), not *mimesis* (imitation): we make sense of the world not through a passive consciousness that reflects a given reality but through an active consciousness that imagines models through which our perceptions of reality cohere: "If one thinks that he imitates external reality, he is deceived, for what one is really doing is imitating his own prior projection (poiesis)." In other words, we live by means of fictions, a word whose Latin root means "to fashion," "to form," "to invent." "Since all our ways of thinking and seeing are our own inventions, formations, and fashionings, there is no such thing as 'nonfiction.' . . . In our fictions are contained our truths."

Jung wrote, "Meaning is something mental or spiritual. Call it a fiction if you like." Meaning is a fiction, but not merely a fabrication. For Jung, the therapist seeks to discover with the patient "the meaning that quickens," "the healing fiction." Not just any story will do. A healing fiction must speak truthfully, giving shape to the reality of the patient's experience. All truths may be fictions (in that they are creative acts of consciousness), but not all fictions are truths. Picasso summed this up nicely when he said that art is "the lie which tells the truth."

For Miller, play is a metaphor for human meaning. But that understates his case. Miller sees play as contemporary culture's central metaphor and as the *mythos* through which society's characteristic sensibilities are expressed. In play we see modeled the process by which we endow experience with meaning, order, beauty, and freedom.

Not all play is sport, but all sport is play. Sport is a narrower category—a type of play. With its closely observed rules of form, sport is less spontaneous than other instances of play and more bound to a society's traditions. The weight of tradition makes sport less suitable than the wider category of play to serve the metaphorical function Miller describes. But if sport falls short as a metaphor for meaning, it succeeds brilliantly as an enactment of it. In sport, the very process of making existence meaningful is distilled, incorporated, and displayed. No wonder, then, that sport can mean so much and so many things. Like art, sport is meaning's self-presentation.

The gods honored and the games played by the ancient Mayans were different from those of the Greeks. But in both cases sport reflected and was a reflection of the culture's "most significant experience of reality." In those cultures, sport's link with the sacred was explicit and ritualized. In ours it is not. Nevertheless, for us, too, sport expresses a reaching for the experience of the sacred. It does so, as it must, in a manner suited to the particular character of our culture.

For us, as for the ancients, sport exists in the borderline realm between jest and earnest. But the nature of that "in-between" place is not stable. It changes in response to the variousness of cultural attitudes and worldviews. For us, the borderline realm is more reflective of a psychological perspective than a cosmological one. Its truths are more metaphoric than literal. The sacred experience it models is based not on theological belief in revealed truth but, as Miller says, on faith in the truth revealed by fiction. Befitting postmodern society's plurality of viewpoints, sport today is laced with a strong dose of irony. And although our world lacks the unifying vision and stability of premodern societies, the second world of sport provides a niche in which mythic consciousness can flourish, allowing us to feel a world graced with depth and meaning. It demonstrates, if not a synthesis of the mythic and rational modes of thought, then a form for their playful interaction. In so doing, sport penetrates our intellectual arrogance and reminds us that, in W. H. Auden's words, "we are lived by powers we pretend to understand." Finally, it teaches us, whether we know it or not, to view this very condition as an expression of the mystery of play. Or as the poet John Webster put it,

> We are merely the stars' tennis balls, struck and bandied
> Which way please them.

CHAPTER FOUR

The Self at Play

> My soul can find no staircase to Heaven unless it be through Earth's loveliness.
>
> MICHELANGELO

Few, if any, have explored the secret life of sport as thoroughly as Michael Murphy, cofounder of the human potential movement's ground zero, Esalen Institute, and author of numerous books dealing with the extraordinary, and largely untapped, capacities within human nature. Indeed, any serious study of sports and spirituality will lead, sooner or later, literally or figuratively, to Murphy's doorstep.

At the time I began researching this book, I wrote him requesting an interview, and his response was prompt and welcoming. Michael Murphy is nothing if not enthusiastic. A few days later, when I arrived at his comfortable, rambling home in Marin County, he greeted me with a hearty handshake—"Hi, Mike Murphy"—and quickly spirited me off in his bronze BMW to a tony restaurant, where we talked over lunch.

In the world of personal growth, Michael Murphy is someone who has seen it, done it, been there. Clearly, he is comfortable with his role as a leading light in the field. His storytelling is polished, his command of facts is impressive, and his observations are deft and intriguing. One notices immediately his easy charm, and a keen, wide-ranging, and hungry intellect. But it is his vision of human possibilities—its breadth, its sheer audacity—that is most striking.

Because of his prominence, Murphy has been the subject of more than a few profiles in books and articles. Those in sympathy with his perspective portray him as a serious scholar cum mystic with a compelling vision of humanity's evolutionary possibilities. On the other hand, the mainstream press tends to regard him as a good-natured, intelligent purveyor of half-baked ideas and flaky lifestyles. Typical of this is a March 1995 *New York Times* piece entitled "A Father of New Age Finds a Divine Reinvention." The author, Bob Morris, never really makes clear what, if anything, this "divine reinvention" entails, but he does manage to get off some zippy one-liners, which seems to be his main concern. Describing Murphy, Morris writes, "Call him in denial, call him terminally positive; he's a man obsessed with getting everyone to the sunny side of the street." Of the early appeal of Esalen's workshops in personal growth, Morris observes, "Referring to total self-involvement as work was a notion whose time had come."

One gets the feeling that Murphy is untroubled by such thick sarcasm. Indeed, he seems to expect it, even to invite it. Murphy is not bashful about his views, and in a culture such as ours, in which "the farther reaches of human nature" don't fit with conventional beliefs about individual identity, ideas that push at the limits of such conventions will at times be met with some hostility. Besides, a degree of skepticism is healthy, sometimes even quite funny. While aboard his forty-foot sloop out in San Francisco Bay, "Mr. Murphy" tells Morris that "we're natural voyagers of body and spirit" and then yells skyward in thanks to God for the beauty of the day, prompting Morris to observe dryly, "He's big on the value of howling into the wind." Mr. Murphy has been howling for a long time.

Murphy was born in 1930 into an affluent middle-class family in Salinas, California. He appears much younger than his years. In his crew-neck sweater, with his dark hair parted neatly on the side, Murphy still has the frat-boy good looks of a Stanford undergraduate. He seems to be in great physical condition, not surprising for someone who in 1984 ran third nationally in the mile for men over fifty. But there is something else. You see it in the spring of his step, the animation of his gestures, and especially in his eyes—they twinkle, boyishly. It is the vision thing—a joyous enthusiasm for exploring the highest human capacities of body, mind, and spirit—that lights him up from within. It is what makes Michael Murphy run.

If one can speak of a starting point of a person's spiritual journey, Murphy's would be during his junior year at Stanford, when he wandered accidentally into a lecture on Eastern religion by the eminent and charismatic Asian scholar Frederic Spiegelberg. As Murphy told Tony Schwartz in *What Really Matters: Searching for Wisdom in America*, hearing Spiegelberg's discussion of Hindu mysticism was "an electrifying event for me, like getting water in the desert. It still stirs me thinking about it. The fact is that I've spent the rest of my life unpacking and developing what I experienced in that first lecture."

The experience set Murphy's life on a new course, one he pursued passionately. The conventions of 1950s college life soon lost their appeal, and he began to devote himself to long hours of meditation and study of Eastern religions. He was particularly drawn to the teachings of the Indian seer Sri Aurobindo Ghose, whose "integral yoga" sought to bring together the insights of yogic mysticism with an evolutionary worldview. "I was taken most with Aurobindo's idea that by your activity in the world [rather than through withdrawal from the world] you could realize divinity. As I heard it, he was saying that evolution is a reflection of the stupendous drama of divinity unfolding within us."

Immersion in the life of the spirit was immensely rewarding. But in time Murphy came to feel acutely a need that was not being met in his mostly solitary practice. In 1956, during his second year of graduate school, well before the international brigades of bohemian seekers made it common to do so, Murphy made his journey to the East, where he studied at the Aurobindo ashram in Pondicherry, India. Aurobindo had died five years earlier, but the ashram continued to thrive, accommodating up to two thousand people at a time. Murphy stayed for a year and a half and was delighted to find that, in keeping with Aurobindo's view that athletics could have a significant place in spiritual life, participation in sports was freely encouraged.

A few years after returning to the States, Murphy hooked up with Richard Price, another Stanford alum, who shared Murphy's passion for exploring the secret life. Seeing the need for a new kind of forum dedicated to, in John Dewey's words, the "education of the whole person," Murphy and Price began to make plans. They envisioned an eclectic environment, one open to a wide range of ideas and practices for unlocking the higher capacities of human potential. In 1962, on a spectacular strip of Big Sur coast that was Murphy family land, the two founded Esalen Institute.

As was to become almost a habit, Murphy's vision was both a step ahead of and deeply in touch with the times. Esalen attracted Aldous Huxley, Gregory Bateson, Alan Watts, Fritz Perls, Margaret Mead, Carl Rogers, and many other such luminaries, who came to teach, talk, hang out, or just soak in the hot baths. For a generation eager to set sail on a voyage of self-discovery away from the sleepy shores of 1950s America, Esalen was catalytic.

But for all the loftiness of the Esalen vision, the real work of running the place was often overwhelming. As thousands flocked to the institute's seminars and workshops, Murphy found himself at the center of a social movement he had scarcely been aware of. As with many a 1960s adventure in consciousness, at Esalen unbridled optimism collided hard and often with brute reality. In Murphy's words, the difficulties of "embodying the higher life while laboring in the lower were becoming ever more apparent."

Stories of God

By 1967, with the summer of love in full bloom, things had gotten old. In his first book, *Golf in the Kingdom*, Murphy wrote: "Thousands of young people from all over the United States were coming down the coast highway looking for some final Mecca of the counter-culture. . . . The air was filled with a drunken mysticism that undermined every discipline we set for the place." He grew weary; then he grew sick, with hepatitis. It was time for a change.

For grounding and renewal, Murphy returned to golf, a game he had grown away from during his journeys Eastward and inward. In younger years, when the only yogi he knew of played catcher for the Yankees, Murphy had been an avid golfer. Every so often, the game would yield up to him an intimation of the transcendent—a self-surpassing performance, a profound moment of joyous and serene clarity. Now he was rediscovering in the game a wellspring of spiritual sustenance. In time, he sought to tell the story of how engaging the soul of the game led to engaging the soul of the man. The result was Murphy's "metaphysical sports fantasy," *Golf in the Kingdom*, published in 1972.

When I asked Murphy about his experience in writing *Golf*, he said, "It seemed to write itself. It was as though I channeled the book in a huge enchantment." That feeling of enchantment permeates the book.

Freely blending autobiography and fantasy, *Golf* tells of a young Murphy's tutelage under Shivas Irons, a mystical master of the Scottish high-country links. With its evocative imagery and lyrical reflections on the game's hidden dimensions, the book tapped into a deep current of common, yet unexpressed, experience. In the March 1993 issue of *Men's Journal* Tom Huth writes:

> The Kingdom fable has developed a cult following over the years. The book has become a bible for students of the inner game, both amateur and professional. Shivas Irons now sells 5,000 copies a month. Among his followers are such pros as John Cook, Peter Jacobsen, Davis Love III, and Tom Watson. . . . Golfers have been writing to [Murphy] as they would to a priest, by the hundreds, confessing their supernatural experiences.

Clearly, enchantment can be contagious. Murphy himself is amazed by the book's success, all of which confirms his belief that the game is a kind of "mystery school for Republicans."

The appeal of *Golf in the Kingdom* continues to grow. Clint Eastwood is planning to make it into a feature motion picture, and some sources mention Sean Connery as the first choice to play the great Irons. When last I spoke with Murphy, in early 1996, he told me that in the previous year, twenty-three years after its initial release, annual book sales had doubled to upward of one hundred thousand. Fascinated by the book's appeal, I decided to look into the matter of its purchase on the soul, though my research was of a decidedly homegrown nature.

Around the time of *Golf*'s publication, my father (not a Republican, but a devoted golfer) read an excerpt in *Sports Illustrated*. Within a few days he went out and bought the book and read it cover to cover. When I recently asked him about the book's draw, he said he was intrigued by what seemed to him the unlikely connection between a mainstream, even elitist, form of recreation and something as significant as deep religious experience. Although my dad was drawn by the story's novel mix of elements, he did not at first imagine that many others would be similarly interested. He says that he is still somewhat puzzled by the book's popularity, but his best guess at an explanation is that it raises to a serious level, and in a sense justifies, an activity to which millions devote huge amounts of energy, time, and money. It reveals the potential for deep meaning in what might otherwise be something of a frivolity.

After my dad read *Golf*, the first person to whom he recommended it was my brother John, with whom he shares a passion for the game. Over the years, John has reread the book numerous times. For him, the key to its charm is the story. He has little interest in the content of Murphy's golf metaphysics, which he dismisses as "watered-down, New Age mysticism." But, he says, Murphy spins a terrific yarn: a wistful, dramatic, and humorous mystical fantasy brimming with spirited optimism. Most of all, John is taken with the relationship at the book's center: that between the young Murphy and his guide into the game's inner life, the mercurial Irons. A lifelong fan of the world's "first consulting detective," John sees parallels with the relationship between Dr. Watson and Sherlock Holmes. Murphy and Watson: the sincere, somewhat wide-eyed chroniclers of extraordinary men, each of whom possesses, in his own way, uncanny insight into the mysterious truth that is obscured by simple appearances.

For my dad and brother both, *Golf in the Kingdom* speaks to those moments when the game evokes a sense of elation, camaraderie, and wholeness of being, the feeling that, contrary to all appearances, something is fundamentally right with the world. Neither of them is much interested in applying Irons's teachings about how to play the inner game, nor do they set much store by Murphy's tales of the superordinary. For both, what they see as the exaggerations of Murphy's fantasy serve to provoke a recognition of the game's more subtle pleasures of the spirit. I suspect that something like this is true for most of *Golf*'s enthusiastic readers. Far more compelling than its tales of things supernatural is the book's knack for eliciting a recognition of a spirit that is simply natural. As Goethe knew, "Mysteries are not necessarily miracles."

As for myself, I was uninterested at first. I had played some golf as a teenager, and the game's charm was lost on me. But that wasn't the main thing. These were for me the early years of Buddhist practice, which I was then pursuing with the kind of devoted and narrow humorlessness that is so common among religious neophytes. The idea of a golf pro cum cosmic sage, for whom the game is a doorway to enlightenment, seemed to me downright silly. When I finally got around to reading the book, however, I found, to my surprise, that I enjoyed it immensely.

As with my brother, it was the story, rather than the ideas, that appealed to me. Rereading it today, I can see John's point about the parallel with Holmes and Watson. But there are other parallels with other books, books that are closer to *Golf* in spirit and substance. In fact, the formal qualities of the *Golf* narrative constitute what has become something of a genre within the literature of that contemporary spiritual renewal that is most often, and most unfortunately, referred to as the New Age.

At the tail end of the 1960s this narrative form was established as a genre within the then-nascent movement because of two of its most influential books: *Be Here Now* by Ram Dass and *The Teachings of Don Juan: A Yaqui Way of Knowledge* by Carlos Casteneda. Despite considerable differences in setting, style, and content, the two (along with the following books in the Don Juan series) are remarkably similar in their structural components. We might call this form the seeker's narrative.

The seeker's narrative is generally a first-person account of a process of spiritual initiation accomplished through the guidance of a master of a tradition of ancient wisdom. Throughout, the style is self-analytic and confessional. At the heart of the story is the relationship between seeker and teacher. The tale typically begins with a serendipitous meeting. The seeker—existentially anguished, well-educated, solidly middle class—is drawn to the master by a strange fascination and vague sense that the master has knowledge of compelling significance. The master, we eventually discover, has recognized some capacity that makes the seeker a potentially worthy vessel to receive that knowledge. As the relationship develops and the seeker enters more fully into the teacher's world, the seeker encounters numerous obstacles, from both without and within. This constitutes the narrative's plot line. The obstacles vary from story to story, but one is a near constant: the sense of cognitive dissonance the seeker experiences in the clash between the reality of the master's world and the logic of the Western rationalist mind-set on which the seeker's ego rests. This tension propels the narrative toward a resolution in which the seeker breaks through the ego's limited vision. Finally, the seeker must return to the world from which he or she came and face the challenge of integrating and sharing the newfound knowledge.

Over the past two or three decades dozens of books have employed this basic form to tell of the authors' apprenticeship with Eastern gurus, South American shamans, Australian aborigines, secret societies, unaffiliated sages, and so forth. They have certainly found a hungry audience. More than a few have recorded sales in the millions, and this despite what is most often predictable storytelling and an unimaginative repackaging of spiritual chestnuts.

But even when poorly told, the seeker's narrative is rich with mythic resonance. One sees, for example, in the various shamans and gurus (almost always men) the archetypal figure Jung called the Wise Old Man. And then there is the search for some secret source of knowledge or blessing, which is one of humankind's most oft told tales—as in, for example, the legend of the Holy Grail. The narrative's archetypal qualities to a large measure account for the appeal of the genre. The form can carry even a poorly realized telling of it. The form has a power all its own.

This is somewhat like the appeal of sport. If we think of a game as a story, the basic elements of its form—rules, roles, objectives, competitive dynamics—are fairly simple. But the form has a certain power that underpins each instance in which it is played out. The predictability of the form yields an unpredictable infinity of ways the game's dramatic elements can rearrange themselves as they build toward the gratification of a resolution that, win or lose, is nonetheless complete. Even those unschooled in the fine points of a sport can find themselves taken in by the sheer inventiveness of the dramatic combination of the simplicity of form and the endless variation in execution.

In a November 1995 *New York Times* article about Woody Allen, the filmmaker speaks at some length about his love of sport, particularly basketball.

> Those Knicks championship teams [in 1969 and 1973],for example, were everything you'd want in the theater and don't usually get. In the theater, you're usually a step ahead of the play or movie. But in sports, it's almost never that way. And those old Knicks—they played such a cerebral, satisfying game. You knew the players, you cared about them, and the drama and tension in the games was fantastic down to the last second.

Allen is a serious and informed student of the game. But his love of sport extends to some pretty remote corners of the sporting world. "I watch [on television] timber-cutting, and rodeos . . . I even know all the rules. I guess in sports it's the combination of competition and athleticism that makes it so interesting to me."

Certainly competition and athleticism are a big part of what draws us to sport. But Allen is also right on the money when he speaks of the attraction of sport's dramatic force and its connection to theater. Indeed, for the spectator, a sporting event can be broken down into the classical elements of a Greek play. First, the setting is established: the place, time, *dramatis personae*, and, in sport, the rules that govern the event. Second is exposition of the problem, the central content of what is to be presented. In an athletic event this includes not only the competitive content but also the background information that tells us what is at stake. Third is the movement of the action toward its climax, and fourth, the resolution.

Like dramatic art, sport embodies the process by which individuals, and whole cultures, establish narrative forms that give shape and meaning to life's chaos of events. We interpret sport through our own deep-seated narratives, the foundations on which we make sense of our lives. In turn, sports nourish individual and collective life by reinvigorating consciousness with the vividness of the stories they display.

In a *New Yorker* piece on the revival of narrative literature, Bill Buford writes: "Strong narrative writing is, at its most elementary, an act of seduction: its object arousal." Much the same can be said of sport. A sporting event draws us into its world, arousing fascination, anticipation, and fierce emotion. Most of all, it incites within us excitement at witnessing human drama stripped down until it shines with an elemental glow.

In their raw dramatics, sports tell of the testing and tempering of the spirit. They are processional enactments of epic themes of women and men confronting the stark solitude at the extremes of exhaustion and despair, of souls embracing the angels and wrestling the demons that dwell in the heights and depths of the human condition, of heroes who find in the self's innermost recesses the key that unlocks the mysterious graces of the human form. Once you are locked into what's going on, the thrill is irresistible.

In sport, again as in dramatic art, while a full realization of the form's potential depends on both the players' mastery and the spectators' active and discerning appreciation, some part of a game's formal and mythic qualities reaches into the soul directly, regardless of our level of expertise.

A favorite illustration of this is in Roger Angell's *Season Ticket*, in which he describes the incredible tension and excitement that seemed to seize the entire city of New York during the sixteen-inning sixth game of the 1986 National League championship series. Following the Mets' victory over the Houston Astros, Angell received a letter from an art critic living in New York's East Village:

> At our apartment during the late innings of Game Six were my
> wife Brooke, our daughter Ada, myself, two dinner guests, and two
> people who had dropped in on short notice and then stayed

around. One of the guests was Nell, a film director we like a lot, even though she's one of those people who can't believe that anyone of your intelligence actually cares about baseball. . . . I don't remember it all, but of course I do remember the growing delirium . . . [like] Nell becoming more and more agitated, and Brooke assuming her old rally posture in a particular doorway we have, and then, at the very end, all the whooping and hollering and inaccurate high-fiving, and some wild hugging. Nell was leaning out the window shrieking with joy.

In *Golf in the Kingdom* Murphy employs the form of the seekers' narrative with great success. Perhaps this is partly because its publication came so soon after *Don Juan* and *Be Here Now*, and the form had a freshness one rarely finds in more recent efforts. But far more important is the quality of the writing and Murphy's knack for striking just the right tone. Writing in the *New Yorker*, John Updike (a publication and a writer as far from the New Age attitudinally as New York is from Esalen geographically) hit the mark in referring to the book's "wit and good will." Murphy tells his tale in a manner that gracefully integrates form and content. The world and the characters he creates are just believable enough, without being too believable. Like myth and like sport, the story rests easily between jest and earnest. Shivas Irons and his home course at Burningbush hover in the mists of imagination, over the next ridge, around the next corner, always just out of reach.

Farther Reaches

One of *Golf*'s early fans was then–San Francisco 49ers quarterback John Brodie. In 1972 Brodie invited Murphy to visit him at the 49ers' training camp, and an *Intellectual Digest* article based on their discussions has become something of a canonical text among those interested in the exceptional experiences athletics can elicit. Unapologetically and matter-of-factly, Brodie describes a kind of heightened reality as being an integral part of an athlete's world.

At times, and with increasing frequency now, I experience a kind of clarity I've never seen adequately described in a football story. Sometimes, for example, time seems to slow way down, in an uncanny way, as if everyone were moving in slow motion. It seems as if I have all the time in the world to watch the receivers run their patterns, and yet I know the defensive line is coming at me just as fast as ever. I know perfectly well how hard and fast those guys are coming and yet the whole thing seems like a movie or a dance in slow motion. It's beautiful.

Like David Meggyesy, Murphy believes that athletes have difficulty incorporating such experiences into their day-to-day lives because they lack a supporting context or philosophy. He writes that "many powerful incidents slip away like Brigadoon because they find no place in the experiencer's ordinary frame of reference," a point with which Brodie, too, agrees:

Football players and athletes generally get into this kind of being or beingness—call it what you will—more often than is generally recognized. But they often lose it after a game or after a season is over. They often don't have a workable philosophy or understanding to support the kind of thing they get into while they are playing. They don't have the words for it. . . . A missing ingredient for many people, I guess, is that they don't have a supporting philosophy or discipline for a better life.

As we speak, Murphy recalls that during his time at the 49ers' camp a number of players told him of their own extraordinary experiences to match those of Brodie: telepathy, prescience, clairvoyance, a sense of being outside one's body, acute well-being, and so forth. Over a few beers one night, a player told Murphy, "Some days there are miracles out there. Yeah, miracles." To illustrate, he spoke of a time he heard a disembodied voice telling him, correctly as it turned out, what was going to happen next. But the next day, when Murphy asked him to say more about it, the player denied any of it had happened, saying he had been drunk and was shooting off his mouth. And he was not alone. Some of the other players also tried to downplay or retract what they had said. It occurred to Murphy that what he was witnessing was a kind of "repression of the sublime."

Repression of the sublime. Obviously, the man has a gift for the bon mot. But his wit is backed up by serious thought and exacting discipline. For Murphy, lifting the veil of this repression is a mission. In numerous publications since *Golf*, he has continued to focus his considerable skills and resources on the awakening of human evolutionary potential. Although *Golf* remains his most popular and accessible work, *The Future of the Body: Explorations into the Further Evolution of Human Nature*, published in 1992, must rank as his most ambitious.

The Future of the Body is a meticulously researched and documented eight-hundred-page encyclopedia of extraordinary human experience, comparable, many have noted, to William James's classic *The Varieties of Religious Experience*. The book is the result of fifteen years of research by the Esalen Institute Study of Exceptional Human Functioning, in which Murphy and his colleagues searched far and wide, across cultures and throughout history, for data—scientific studies, witness reports, and personal accounts—that would illuminate the human capacity for radical transformation.

> Like the unassembled pieces of a great jigsaw puzzle, discoveries about our developmental possibilities are scattered across the intellectual landscape, isolated from one another in separate fields of inquiry. . . . By gathering data from many fields—including medical science, anthropology, sports, the arts, psychical research, and comparative religious studies—we can identify extraordinary versions of most, if not all, of our basic attributes.

The Future of the Body is a kind of natural history of the metanormal. Twelve human attributes—communication abilities, vitality, cognition, movement abilities, capacities to manipulate the environment directly, volition, somatic awareness and self-regulation, perception of external phenomena, feelings of pain and pleasure, sense of self, love, and bodily structures—are identified, and evidence of extraordinary functioning is offered for each. Clairvoyance, for example, would be a case of extraordinary cognition; an ego-transcendent experience is a metanormal version of the sense of self. Though his claims are lofty indeed, Murphy backs them up with a tremendous wealth of examples for each case. For instance, the well-documented abilities of martial arts masters to develop and channel *ki*, the body's vital energy, is cited to demonstrate the capacity for extraordinary vitality. Scientific studies of yoga adepts who can control their pulse and heartbeat, body temperature, and brain wave patterns are cited as evidence of extraordinary somatic awareness and self-regulation.

Obviously, one cannot accept all testimony about such matters while claiming scientific validity.

> For an inquiry as wide-ranging as this, we must be bold and yet employ the critical distance that characterizes good science. In this empirical spirit, we can divide supposed metanormalities into three categories: first, those, such as spiritual healing, that have been reported again and again in many cultures and that have been verified by good tests of their authenticity; second, those, such as telekinesis, for which we do not have certain evidence but which nevertheless are supported by testimonies that are hard to dismiss; and third, those for which there is little or no support. In this book, I reject members of the third class but do consider members of the second.

From the mountain of data emerges a map of the furthest reaches of human functioning. But the map is not the end; it is the means to finding the extraordinary in our common life. In Murphy's view, these extraordinary capacities can be cultivated by anyone. In the last section of the book, Murphy turns his attention to outlining the transformative practices through which ordinary people can realize their own exceptional potential.

Not surprisingly, Murphy draws heavily from the world of sports. As he said to me, "Modern sports push people in ways we have never been pushed before. They are a vast laboratory for exploring extraordinary life." Sport dramatizes the richness of physical life and our capacity to surpass apparent limits. Like a spiritual practice, sport trains one to focus the energies of mind and body, which can, in turn, awaken the self to its deeper dimensions. Indeed, for Murphy, "Sports are our very own Western yoga, a vehicle for lifting the common life to divine heights."

Such musings may sound far-fetched, even for the most ardent sports enthusiast. But even if Murphy is correct when he claims that "our secret tendency, our *telos*, is to manifest divine nature in the flesh," the question remains, Why sports? I mean, why not just do the things mystics have always done—meditation or yoga or whatever?

As a matter of fact, Murphy asked a similar question of Brodie: Why look to football as a way of developing higher human possibilities? To which Brodie responded, Well, why not? Why set limits on what the game can be about? "I see no reason why we should fix the game of football where it is, after the change it has gone through already. Why shouldn't it be a place to develop the mental and spiritual dimensions we have been talking about?"

But today, Murphy's attitude about the spiritual role of sport seems more urgent. "We don't have good ways into those higher states of being. Contemplative systems work only for the most gifted, and failure to grow means that the self becomes stunted." Murphy cites the psychologist Abraham Maslow's notion of the Jonah complex, the idea that we are afraid of our greatest good. In *The Farther Reaches of Human Nature* Maslow wrote:

> We fear our highest possibilities (as well as our lowest ones). We are generally afraid to become that which we can glimpse in our most perfect moments, under the most perfect conditions, under conditions of greatest courage. We enjoy and even thrill to the Godlike possibilities we see in ourselves in such peak moments.

And yet we simultaneously shiver with weakness, awe and fear before these very same possibilities.

In Murphy's view, "Denial of our evolutionary capacities causes them to stagnate within us or erupt in a painful or distorted way. Both individually and as a species, we either grow or die."

At the conclusion of our two-hour interview, the extravagance of Murphy's reflections left me a bit lightheaded. Whatever one makes of Murphy's grand speculations—and I am skeptical of many of them—the sheer weight of hard evidence and sound thinking out of which they emerge constitutes a formidable challenge to modernity's conventional notions of the boundaries of human experience. What is most compelling about Murphy is not the answers he provides but the questions he provokes—questions like, Can we afford *not* to open to our larger possibilities? To ask such things, to wonder about them, and to explore that wonder to its fullest—this is, I suspect, Murphy's real game.

Murphy has illuminated the spiritual potential of sport with an enthusiasm that is contagious. Among the many books addressing sport's inner life, his influence is singularly pervasive. Like most visionary efforts, Murphy's work is often more successful at freeing us to imagine what might be than at connecting us with what actually is. Throughout history, grand visions of human destiny have rarely come to pass. The same power that propels a vision forward—the capacity to hold together in its orbit fantasies, insights, facts, and longings—also works to blind those who hold it to the partiality of their own perspective. A vision runs into problems when it fails to include a recognition that it is less a revelation of truth than a means by which we can play at truth.

The problem is illustrated when we compare *Golf in the Kingdom* to *The Future of the Body*. Written twenty years apart, the two books share a strong thematic continuity, though in tone and attitude they are worlds apart. The difference takes us back to some distinctions addressed in the previous chapter: mythic consciousness versus rational consciousness, the imaginative reality of sport's second world versus the purposive reality of everyday experience, fictive truths that give events meaning versus literal truths that give causal explanation.

Both books bear the strong stamp of the thought of Sri Aurobindo, particularly his vision of evolution as the progressive manifestation of Divinity in the physical world. But the ideas in *Golf* speak most strongly as myths and metaphors that quicken one's sense of the secret life. *Future*, on the other hand, is primarily a work of natural science. Its ideas must be taken at face value; its truth claims must be measured against a factual, rather than an experiential, yardstick.

In *Future* Murphy makes a compelling argument for our metanormal potential. In doing so he calls into question many of our culture's assumptions about human nature. No doubt, some of his claims and a fair amount of his evidence will wilt upon closer scrutiny. But skepticism—that is, open-minded and self-critical skepticism—will, I think, ultimately strengthen the core of his argument.

The strength of *Future* is the thoroughness with which Murphy gathers and presents information anomalous to material science's view of the capacities of the human organism. Murphy is at his best when he lets the evidence speak for itself. He is less persuasive in fitting the material within his overall interpretive framework. In interpreting our metanormal capacities as indicators of humanity's evolutionary destiny, Murphy takes a huge jump, one that is certainly open to question.

Murphy is among those who ascribe to evolution a sensible directionality, which they see as a movement toward increased complexity and greater consciousness. This perspective is rejected by many evolutionary thinkers, including Stephen Jay Gould (who is, incidentally, also an eminent baseballologist), who dismisses it as a "spin-doctored" view. But it is not my intention, nor am I even qualified, to enter into this debate. It is the power of the idea of evolution that is pertinent to our present concerns.

If we set aside questions of the merits of competing theories, the power of the idea remains, for evolution is our creation story. When Murphy places sport within the framework of evolution, he is following a tradition going back to prehistory of linking sport to the larger designs of the cosmos. The Mayans, for example, saw their ball games as enactments of their creation story, and through them humans assumed their rightful place in the structure of the cosmos. Similarly, by tying sport to the evolutionary movement of the cosmos, Murphy frames sport as a means by which we fulfill our role in the grand drama of creation's unfolding. The story that is sport and the story of the cosmos are bound together. Whether or not it is a good science, Murphy's vision works as mythic narrative. Although he uses the ideas and language of science, the meaning he seeks reveals itself, as it must, as myth.

It is natural, perhaps inevitable, that we should seek in the idea of evolution a connection between the scientific realm of causal explanation and the experiential realm of human meaning. But in doing so, evolution is no longer only a fact of science; it is also a metaphor with mythic significance. And while sport can and should be inclusive of science, its intrinsic mode of consciousness is inextricably bound up with myth. Sport can use science, but it needs myth.

When Shivas Irons describes *true gravity*—the central term in his mystical lexicon and the key to entering golf's spiritual dimensions—as a means of aligning oneself with the emerging will of God, or "the next manifesting plane" as he calls it, it really doesn't matter whether this is sound evolutionary thought. He is speaking the language of the second world and evoking directly the joy of being astonished by existence. And whatever the merits of *Future*'s evolutionary vision, its thorough and rich discussion of the extraordinary nature of human potential speaks similarly to the thrill of recognizing our capacity to surpass expectations, to the ecstasy of shattering apparent limits, and to the burn of the "hard, gem-like flame" of self-transcendence.

An Intrinsic Good

Murphy's view that sport constitutes a Western yoga is widely shared by those who write about the relationship between sport and spirituality (George Leonard in the *Ultimate Athlete* and Timothy Gallwey in *The Inner Game of Tennis*, to name two). I've always found something troubling about this line of thinking, though it has taken years to flesh out my understanding of why this should be so.

During the years I lived at the Zen Center, I was part of a coterie of ten or so hardcore sports devotees. We were a loosely knit group, and others joined in freely as the spirit moved them. In particular, certain special occasions—a crucial World Series game, the Superbowl—would widen our circle, and sometimes our ranks would swell in number several times over. My most vivid memory of this was when one of our inner circle, Chuck Davis, arranged for the pay-per-view reception of the second Sugar Ray Leonard–Roberto Duran fight. As it happened, the match was to occur on the night of Maezumi Rōshi's weekly lecture. In the upstairs of the building next to the *zendō* (meditation hall) was a small commons room with a TV set, and on fight night about forty of us crammed ourselves in there like frat kids in a phone booth. Some, myself included, came dressed—disguised, really—in our meditation robes, so our comings and goings would go undetected. I was later told that Rōshi expressed surprise at all the zendō's empty seats and that he was visibly puzzled by the sound of cheers that, despite our attempts to muffle them, erupted periodically.

Most often, however, our athletic pleasures were far less guilty, and we indulged them within the proper limits of the rules of training. On days off, we would, on occasion, join in a softball game at a nearby park, and more than a few folks jogged for health. But basketball was the game of choice. We set up a terrific hoop in the parking lot behind the administrative building, and during the break before dinner you were likely to spot a small group of us shooting around, hanging out, and (as the Hawaiians say) talking story. Pickup games were usually reserved for days off, and sometimes they got pretty serious.

During roughly this same period—mid-1970s to mid-1980s—books applying spirituality to athletics were at the height of their popularity. But oddly, I cannot recall a single conversation with other Buddhist sports fans about such books. I guess no one had much interest in the idea of using sport as a spiritual path. I certainly did not. Even my affection for *Golf in the Kingdom* was based more on a playful reading of its imaginative spirit than on a serious reading of its literal content.

For me, and I think for my Buddhist cohorts, one of the pleasures of sport was that it offered respite from the weighty introspection of Zen training. This is not to say that we rejected the notion that participation in sport could in some way enrich the inner life. But our disinterest, I think, reflected a certain skepticism about approaching sport as Zen by another name. We shared a recognition, intuitive and largely unspoken, that sport has a basis that is intrinsically its own and is distinct from that of a meditative path. Also unspoken and, at least for me, unconscious was a sense that to sully that difference by approaching sport as a kind of yoga was to diminish sport by placing it in a context with which it has no organic relationship.

In *The Joy of Sport* Michael Novak addresses matters of this sort in a chapter aptly titled "Sports are not 'The Game of Life.'" Novak cites Aristotle's assertion that wisdom dictates that each sphere of life be seen in its proper measure. "Each sphere," writes Novak, "is unique. Each has its own proper conditions, laws, and contexts." Indeed, failure to discern the uniqueness of each of life's realms is a "sin of intellect."

For Novak, sports delight us because they are *not* the Game of Life, because they offer liberty from the encumbrance of life's practical concerns. Sports are good in themselves. They are natural expressions of the energies native to human life. They need not be justified in accordance with purposes that are not their own.

The virtues cultivated and expressed in sport have an ambiguous relationship to virtues in other realms of activity. How a society mediates this relationship exerts a tremendous influence on the way sports are perceived, the forms they take, and the meanings they are assigned. One of the recurring themes in the history of sport in the West is the tension between, on the one hand, the view that the value of athletic expression is intrinsic and self-evident and, on the other, the attitude that the worth of sport must be proved in serving the practical and moral standards set by the broader society.

The issue is well illustrated by contrasting the place of sport in the societies of ancient Greece and Rome. For the Greeks, athletics celebrated the sanctity of the human condition. Sport enriched the soul and expressed the fulfillment of human development. Though the Romans absorbed much of Greek culture, their attitude toward sport was markedly different. Many Romans feared that the homoeroticism of Greek athletics would be a corrupting influence on young Roman men. But even greater was the fear that the ethos of Greek athletics—individualistic, highly aesthetic, unconcerned with practical (particularly military) application— would undermine the formation of the competent and obedient soldiers needed to serve the empire.

The Romans, of course, loved sport, but they did so in a manner entirely their own. The Greek ideal of excellence (*arete*) achieved through struggle (*agon*) did not suit Roman tastes. Roman games were primarily entertainment, a means of diverting the populace from the causes of possible social unrest. In Juvenal's classic formula, sports were the circuses the Roman masses craved along with their bread. Not surprisingly, the games most favored by Rome were brutal spectacles of the sort made famous in the Colosseum: gladiatorial bouts, chariot races, and animal combat.

To the Greeks, the brutality of Roman games was one reason among many to regard Romans as barbaric people. But the most potent criticism of the games came from the early Christians. To

some extent, Christian opposition was simply a practical matter—
no one, after all, likes being the unwilling object of others' amuse-
ments, especially when this entails being chased down and
devoured by lions. Practical concerns notwithstanding, Christian
opposition was based most strongly on moral grounds, on abhor-
rence of the games' cruelty and their connection to worldly politics
and ambition.

Early Christians were, however, more favorably disposed
toward the Greek games. Indeed, Saint Augustine wrote that Christians "ought not to reject a good thing because it is pagan. God is
the author of all things. To continue the good customs that have
been practiced by idolaters . . . is not to borrow from them; on the
contrary, it is taking from them what is not theirs and giving it to
God, the real owner." This attitude was adopted, though not without some dissent, by medieval Christians toward the pagan sports
of pre-Christian Europe.

In France, ball games became an essential feature of Easter
ceremonies. William J. Baker, in his highly readable *Sports in the
Western World*, writes of how in the city of Auerre "colorfully garbed
church officials formed a processional down the aisle of the church.
Chanting a traditional liturgy, they danced to the music of an Easter hymn while passing a ball from person to person."

Unintentionally, the example of the church contributed to the
popularization and proliferation of forms of ball playing. But the
church took an active hand as well, encouraging parishioners in ball
games and other forms of recreation, even making church property
available for the purpose.

In time the spread of ball games into the mainstream of
medieval life met with a backlash. By the late Middle Ages the
games of the common folk were under attack by leaders of both
church and state. (Not surprisingly, the aristocracy were largely left
unbothered.) Sports were denounced on moral grounds for being
dangerous, rancorous, and socially disruptive. But, as in Rome centuries earlier, the main objection was that they distracted young

men from preparing themselves in the skills of warfare. But despite such pronouncements from on high, the ball, so to speak, had been set rolling, and the peasantry resisted with stubbornness and pride attempts to deny them their games.

The sports culture of the common folk was dealt another harsh blow by the Protestant Reformation. Although Martin Luther was himself a robust proponent of sport, not all the Reformation's leaders followed suit. John Calvin, in particular, took a dim view of games—as he did of most everything. Following Calvin, the English Puritans railed against "devilish pastimes" and, as they gained political power, sought to legislate against them. In *The Anatomy of Abuses*, written in 1581, the Puritan divine Philip Stubbes expressed the pious sentiment that "any exercise which withdraws us from godliness, either upon the sabbath or any other day, is wicked, and to be forbidden." In true Puritan fashion, Stubbes left little room for debate on the issue.

In time the pendulum swung back. With the Stuart Restoration in 1660, Puritan influence, including their discouragement of sport, declined. Britons returned to their playing fields in a long rush of enthusiasm. In the American colonies, despite Puritanism's formative influence, a distinctive sports culture was growing from the recreations European settlers brought with them from their various points of origin. The settlers also encountered among their new homeland's native inhabitants cultures in which the passionate pursuit of sport was integral to social life. The settlers recognized marked similarities between ball games of the Indians and their own. But, sadly, they didn't know what to make of the religious rituals that surrounded Indian sports, for European sport had long since been secularized. As Baker notes, had the Europeans known their own history of linking sport to the sacred "they would have recognized their own past in the Indians' present."

Sport was not exempt from the massive changes brought by the Industrial Revolution. The rapid growth of cities created the need for new forms of recreation that were suited to urban life.

Sports clubs, school teams, and the like provided a sense of social connection to counter the anonymity of city and factory. Like the factories in which they worked, the games people played became highly organized. As in the factories, technology played an ever-increasing role in shaping the sports landscape. Advances in technology expedited transportation to sporting events, stirred up interest through increased communication, and made necessary equipment more available. The Industrial Revolution gave rise to mass leisure, and with it, sport reached a level of prominence it had never before attained as a secular activity. Over the past century and a half, its prominence has only increased.

Although the athletic culture of today is in many ways historically unique, it is shadowed by issues that have followed sport through the centuries: debates about its moral effects, its proper role in society, and the values it embodies. Struggles over these issues, past and present, concern not only the forms and functions of sport but also—and most deeply—its meaning. These struggles of the past are not only sports history; they are also sport's legacy.

It is not difficult, for example, to see in today's mass sporting events the circuslike atmosphere of the brutal entertainments of Rome. But other elements of the past may be more difficult to discern. Sport has, so to speak, vanquished its institutional opponents. Today, many of the views of the past opposing sport have been incorporated into the logic of its culture. In a kind of ideological twist on the old saw, if you can't beat 'em, join 'em, what were once reasons to condemn sport have been reworked into arguments for the virtue of sport. Athletics are no longer seen as a hindrance to military preparation but as an aid to it. Rather than be rejected because of its moral effects, sport is now embraced for its beneficial role in moral formation.

In contradistinction to the sort of utilitarian thinking that would see sport as a means to a higher end is the view, epitomized by the Greeks, that the value of sport is immanent in the very qualities that provide its deepest satisfactions: the natural grace it expresses; the intelligence and skill it elicits; the intensity, richness, and order with which it imbues experience. Sport maintains these values regardless of how well it delivers on the extrinsic values with which it is continually saddled. Whether or not it is recognized and whether or not it is given articulation, this sacred dimension is ever present and irreducible. But recognizing and articulating sport's intrinsic virtue also holds value in itself, because doing so enhances and brings into consciousness the vitality of athletic culture and play.

Whereas the frowning Puritans of old decried the wickedness of sport for turning us from God's holy precincts, an updated style of Puritan thinking applies the same logic in reverse, extolling the goodness of sport as an instrument of moral betterment. Its proponents assert that sport builds character, provides moral lessons, and makes us better players in the Great Game of Life. I fear that to approach sport as a form of yoga is simply to give a New Age twist to this religious utilitarianism. Sport is, again, a means to extrinsic ends, this time called higher consciousness, self-realization, or enlightenment. As I've been arguing, sport does indeed spirit us godward, but it does so on its own terms and in its own way.

Of the many guidebooks in the use of sport as a means of spiritual realization, the most successful, both in popularity and quality, is W. Timothy Gallwey's *The Inner Game of Tennis*. Despite my quarrel with its sport-as-yoga premise, I think it is a fine book. Gallwey is a talented teacher, and his writing is clear and insightful. He does a terrific job describing the ways certain mental processes interfere with one's play and then adapting rudimentary psychological and meditative techniques for overcoming these self-induced obstacles. It is a great book for improving one's game. But the mere use of spiritual techniques does not a yoga make.

In some significant ways, Gallwey anticipates the findings of Susan Jackson, discussed in chapter 2, on the flow experience among athletes. Gallwey writes that the inner game "is played against such obstacles as lapses in concentration, nervousness, self-doubt, and self-condemnation"—exactly the states of mind most likely to interfere with flow and peak performance. Gallwey and Jackson even use the same term to describe the quality most valuable to an athlete in reaching the optimal state of mind: relaxed concentration.

There is nothing new about applying the concentrative techniques of meditation outside the traditional contexts in which they evolved. Maezumi Rōshi, for example, like most any Zen master, spoke on occasion about how the skills of meditation can be used to such ends as improving one's health, reducing stress, or creating a sense of well-being. In Japan it has even become common corporate practice to send young executives to Zen monasteries for a week or two to encourage greater discipline and group cohesion. But all this is a far cry from practice undertaken within the context of *butsudō*, the buddha way. In his book *The Mind of Clover* Robert Aitken Rōshi, the most revered of Western-born Zen masters, writes:

> Spiritual knowledge is a powerful tool. Certain teachings of Zen
> Buddhism and certain elements of its practice can be abstracted
> and used for secular purposes, some of them benign, such as
> achievement in sports; some nefarious, such as murder for hire.
> The Buddha Dharma with its integration of wisdom and compassion must be taught in its fullness.

To get a better handle on what is at issue here, it might be helpful to distinguish between the methods one employs and the approach one takes in practicing a discipline, whether it be neurosurgery, Afro-Cuban dance, baseball, or Zen Buddhism. *Method* refers to the foreground of practice, to the techniques and technical knowledge one applies in a given field of activity. *Approach* refers to something broader and less concrete. It is the background of practice, comprising such things as attitudes, ideals, goals, assumptions, and emotional tone. Approach provides a framework that governs and holds together the meanings of particular acts and ideas. Methods can be specified clearly and taught systematically. But the elements of approach are usually transmitted by less direct means. They are absorbed in the process of living within a discipline. They often operate beneath the threshold of consciousness. They belong less to the self than to their own history and traditions.

A pitcher refines his mechanics, works on the placement of his pitches, studies the strengths and weaknesses of the batters he will face, and so forth. A Zen Buddhist does zazen, directing her attention to her breath and posture and allowing her thoughts to pass freely into and out of consciousness. Pitching a baseball and doing zazen both require skill in relaxed concentration, and in that sense they share a degree of foreground similarity. But they both emerge from and feed into backgrounds that are vastly different. And even should that pitcher undertake the practice of zazen to help his focus when pitching, that differentness remains.

An examination, even a cursory one, of a discipline's core terminology reveals much about the background of that field of endeavor. Such core terms signify far more than is contained within a definition; indeed, they tend to carry an entire culture of meaning. The word *yoga* is a pertinent example.

The literal meaning of the Sanskrit *yoga* is "yoke," in the sense in which two things are joined and brought into union. *The Shambhala Dictionary of Buddhism and Zen* tells us that in Hinduism *yoga* "has the sense of harnessing oneself to God, seeking union with the Divine."

In the *Yoga-Sutra*, Patañjali, the great second-century systematizer of yogic thought, defined yoga as "control of the fluctuations of the stuff of the mind." The system outlined by Patañjali comprises eight steps. The first two concern proper moral conduct; the next three involve training the body in posture, breath control, and withdrawal of the senses from external objects; and steps six through eight refer to the meditative cultivation of consciousness that leads to the realization of ultimate unity, the deepest experience of reality.

In the West yoga is often thought of solely as the bodily exercises of step three. Such thinking is problematic not only because it refers to just a small part of the range of yogic technique but also because it barely scratches the surface of the background, the approach, in which the techniques are embedded: philosophical assumptions and attributions of value to such matters as the nature of consciousness and its relationship to the body, the emotions, and the contents of thought; human purposes and ethics; the nature of everyday experience and divine reality and the relationship between the two; the appropriate mode and attitude for the transmission of yogic knowledge; the connection, if any, between historical processes and the experience of ultimate reality; and the list goes on. Pervasive to the entire yogic enterprise is the idea that the highest of human goals is that transformation of consciousness that leads to divine union.

Although yoga is rooted deeply in Hindu tradition, the term was taken up by Buddhists, who adapted and applied it to their own meditative practices. Indeed, one of the most influential schools of Indian Buddhism was called Yogāchāra, which translates literally as "application of yoga." But the term applies more broadly still. The *yoga* entry in Shambhala's dictionary addresses this point as it continues: "As a way to knowledge of Truth, yoga in its broadest sense is not confined to India. All seekers for the experience of fundamental unity (the so-called mystical experience), whether they are Indian shamans or Christian mystics, are yogis in this sense."

A term less familiar to Westerns than *yoga* but no less rich in its implications for the spiritual life is the Japanese word *butsudō*, "buddha way." The Asian cultures in which Buddhism has flourished have no term truly equivalent to the English *Buddhism*. In East Asia, the term used most often is buddha way. *Butsu* is Japanese for *buddha*, a Sanskrit word whose literal meaning is "awakened one." The word applies to the historical figure Shakyamuni Buddha, to various cosmic buddhas, and to buddhas of past ages and future ones. *Buddha* is also a synonym for the nondual reality to which a buddha has fully awakened. It also describes the essential nature of all beings, who are, whether they know it or not, themselves buddhas. That is, buddhas and nonbuddhas are endowed with the same buddha nature; the only difference is that a buddha is "awake" to that fact.

The second part of the term is *dō*, which is Japanese for the Chinese *tao*, "the way." "The way" may refer to the originative or ordering principle of the cosmos, to a state of harmony based on that principle, to a path for achieving that harmony, or to the content of the harmony achieved. *Butsudō*, then, is the way of awakening to and harmonizing with one's true nature. In Japan, *dō* is applied to the various Zen-inspired "ways" of training, such as *chadō* (the way of tea), *kendō* (the way of the sword), and *kyudō* (the way of the [archer's] bow).

In *The Zen Way to the Martial Arts* Taisen Deshimaru Rōshi reasserts a point made by countless others: the essence of Japan's martial ways is not technical mastery but self-mastery.

> In Japanese, *do*, means the way. How do you walk on this way? How can you find it? It is not just learning a technique, still less is it a sporting match. Budo includes such arts as *kendo, judo, aikido,* and *kyudo* or archery; yet the ideogram *bu* also means to cease the struggle. In Budo the point is not only to compete, but to find peace and mastery of the self.

Still less is it a sporting match. One could hardly ask for a clearer refutation of the kind of thinking that would make of sport a spiritual path simply by highlighting its concentrative elements and reframing some of its ideas. And Deshimaru Rōshi is hardly alone. With one or two exceptions, all the masters of Zen, yoga, the martial arts, and so forth that I've ever come across are pretty much of like mind. These disciplines are not games. They differ from sport not only in form but also in approach.

Oddly enough, however, spiritual teachers like Deshimaru Rōshi and exponents of sport as a kind of yoga are in basic agreement on a fundamental point, which is their conception of what constitutes a spiritual life. Zen masters are right when they say sport is not a "way," but they are mistaken, I believe, in therefore dismissing sport for lacking spirituality. Inner game enthusiasts are correct in seeing that sport is an abundant wellspring of spiritual life, but they err when they impose upon sport an inner logic that is not its own.

Eros and Excellence

The task of discerning the inner logic of the approach of sport is more difficult than doing so with a spiritual path. By their nature, spiritual traditions regard self-knowledge as a necessary virtue and explicit goal, and so, inevitably, they concern themselves with developing and bringing into conscious awareness the elements that characterize their approach. But in sport self-knowledge is not a virtue of significant measure. If an athlete's culture does not provide her with a link between her activity and its deepest sources of meaning, that background may go largely unnoticed, for sport provides no intrinsic impetus for the athlete to inquire into the paradigmatic elements from which her craft is constituted. One may compete in a sport for a lifetime and never seriously consider the deep assumptions and values that shape and guide its practice. Nevertheless, the matter of approach is as essential to the experience of sport as it is to any other serious pursuit, and as in other pursuits, much of the background of sport is revealed by its core terms.

Some of this territory has been examined in previous chapters. In contrast to the equanimity, detachment, and directionality of a meditative path, the secret life of sport thrives on enthusiasm (a word whose Greek source means "possessed by a god"), on both player and fan being carried away (*desporto*) into a more vital mode of being. The spirituality of sport is rooted in a primitive—that is, primary—sensibility of the sacred: ecstatic, communal, nonpro-grammatic, and linked to potent natural forces.

Our word for the one who plays a sport, the athlete, derives from the Greek *athlein*, "to contend for a prize." Although richer rewards were not uncommon, a wreath of olive branches, the prize in question, was of modest material value. The real worth of the prize lay in what it signified: the attainment and display of majesty in the human body and soul. The fulfillment of human virtue was demonstrated in the *agon* (conflict, contest, struggle) of the athlete. That the same word, *agon*, referred to both an athletic contest and a military engagement speaks of the ferocity with which athletes competed. We get a sense of this from Homer's description of a wrestling match, in which the participants' backs "fairly creaked as they gripped each other's hands with their hands and grappled for all they were worth, streaming with sweat and raising many a blood-livid welt on each other's ribs and shoulders as both of them strained every muscle." No surprise, then, that our own word *agony* derives from the experience of athletes competing.

To compete, "to seek together," is to pursue virtue in the extremes—in the agonies and in the ecstasies—of human experi-ence. For the Greeks, the virtue underpinning all others displayed in the *agon*—courage, heart, endurance, presence of mind, physical mastery—was *arete*, "excellence," the preeminent human ideal.

The religious historian Mircea Eliade writes that, for the Greeks of antiquity, the condition of humans was seen to be pre-carious, fragile, and delimited by *moira*, the "portion" of life allotted to one by the gods. But this tragic vision, rather than leading to despair, served to stimulate the Greek religious genius to discover perfection and sanctity in the finitude of natural existence. A wise and noble life was one lived fully, yet virtuouşly, in the present. Through their consciousness of the limits imposed by the gods on human existence, the Greeks, writes Eliade, "rediscovered and brought to the full the religious sense of the 'joy of life,' the sacra-mental value of erotic experience and of the beauty of the human body, the religious function of every organized collective occasion for rejoicing—processions, games, dances, singing, sports competitions, spectacles, banquets, etc."

Athletic competitions were occasions to display and contemplate the elements of excellence in the human form: balance, proportion, rhythm, harmonious movement, strength, speed, agility. *Arete* provided one with a glimpse of something more fundamentally beautiful and real than what was apparent in the natural datum of everyday experience. Excellence demonstrated the perfection of the human body and the sanctity of the human condition.

The Greeks' sense of the religious nature of sport was tied to the power of *eros* that sport embodied. In the *Symposium* Plato (who, by the way, trained under Athens's foremost wrestling teacher, and whose original name, Aristocles, was changed by his teacher to Plato, "broad shouldered") writes that the highest erotic passion was the "divine delirium," the ecstasy of delight in beauty. Obviously, such erotic passion had a much broader meaning than just sexual energy. Eros, love, was a principle, a primal, religious drive to participate in life's perfection. In *Love in the Western World* Denis de Rougemont writes: "Plato linked Love and Beauty, although what he called Beauty was above all the intellectual essence of uncreated perfection—the form of all excellence."

Now we can understand more clearly the spiritual significance of *arete*. By illustrating perfect beauty, excellence transported the soul in a religious rapture. In the *Phaedrus* Plato writes of "the shudder that runs through" the soul in the recognition of divine beauty and of the "old awe" that steals over one in the throes of the experience. In excellence life reveals its divine majesty.

Although contemporary Western culture is largely descended from ancient Greece, we are, as Nietzsche observed, far less "Greek" than we imagine. The significance we ascribe to excellence illustrates this point well. Excellence is for us certainly a virtue, perhaps even an ideal, but it is a fairly pedestrian one. Accomplishment, success, a high level of performance—these are all admirable, of course, but there is little here to connect excellence with the wellsprings of divinity. Although we may be lacking in ideas that would express this connection, we feel it nonetheless. It is structured into human experience. Whether or not we assign to it sacred significance, excellence, *arete*, retains the capacity to awaken in us a sense of the sacred, to reveal, in Eliade's words, that which is "real, powerful, rich, and meaningful."

Using words that recall Plato's own, Paul Weiss opens his *Sport: A Philosophic Inquiry* with the observation:

> Excellence excites and awes. It pleases and it challenges. We are often delighted by splendid specimens whether they be flowers, beasts, or men. A superb performance interests us even more because it reveals to us the magnitude of what then can be done. Illustrating perfection, it gives us a measure for whatever else we do.

There are, Weiss notes, many areas in life in which a person may attain excellence: in character, in knowledge, in artistic achievement, and so forth. But for the young especially, sport is the "most promising" means for such attainment. Furthermore, for young and old, athlete and spectator, sport has a singular power to disclose excellence and to evoke the ecstasy and awe afforded by a glimpse of perfection. In the same vein, Michael Novak writes that in sport, "a great play is a revelation. The curtains of ordinary life part, and perfection flashes for an instant before the eye."

Sport approaches the sacred not by means of a spiritual path, a way, but through the eros of excellence. The formal limits of sport give the excellence it displays an accessibility and luminosity greater than is found in most any other field of endeavor, where the relationships among meaning, purpose, and action are more diffuse and complicated. An athletic event is a container constituted of well-defined boundaries, clear rules and objectives, and simple forms that allow the chaos of life to be distilled, given shape, and polished, until it radiates what John Updike wrote of as "the hard blue glow of high purpose." Whether one participates in it as a player or spectator, the elemental world of the *agon* enriches the soul, and nature itself, by its revelation through *arete* of natural perfection.

But such talk of excellence and perfection can mislead us as to their place in the secret life. Perfection may suggest only a form, but not the process through which that form is realized. When we speak of excellence, we generally mean an objectively high level of performance, not the subjectively full realization of one's abilities, whatever their level may be. But excellence and perfection belong not only to the realm of external standards but also to the realm of experience, in which they are universal. Inwardly, they belong to us all.

This recalls Hans-Georg Gadamer's notion of "deep play," which I referred to in chapter 2. In deep play the individual's actions so thoroughly merge with the intrinsic designs of the game that the game plays the player. No doubt this experience occurs with greater frequency and is more evident and impressive among expert athletes. But excellence and perfection do not belong to the player; they belong to the game itself. And anyone who has felt himself given over to their power—the Little League pitcher, the junior varsity linebacker, the weekend softball player, or the devoted fan—has come to share in some measure of the experience.

In distinguishing sport's approach to the sacred from those of spiritual disciplines, my intent has been to bring into sharper focus the particular character of sport's religious function. By seeing what sport is not, we see more clearly what in fact it is. Sport has its own footing in the secret life, and failure to appreciate this fact diminishes the spirit of athletic play.

This is not to say that there are not significant resemblances between sport and other modes of spiritual enrichment—religious, artistic, psychological, and otherwise. Indeed, in matters of the inner life, clearly drawn distinctions, though necessary, are often as not, also deceptive. Language, by its nature, can produce a conceptual clarity that is untrue to lived experience. In the individual's process of living out separate disciplines, the boundary between the spiritual life of sport and that of yoga, Zen, or the martial arts may be quite fuzzy and frayed. Differences in meaning often blur and at times disappear altogether, as two fields of activity are integrated into the wholeness of one's experience.

Powers beyond the Self

The experience of Japanese baseball's magnificent home-run champion Sadaharu Oh, which I discussed briefly in chapter 2, illustrates this point well. Oh's intensive training in the principles of aikidō and kendō certainly helped his hitting tremendously. But in "applying the Japanese psyche to an American game," baseball, he writes, became "everything"—that is, through the single-minded love and pursuit of his discipline, he experienced an inward fruition of the spirit, the effects of which extended to all aspects of his life.

Oh had the advantage of being part of a culture with a long tradition of transforming secular activities—arranging flowers, serving tea, engaging an opponent in combat—into "ways" for the cultivation of the spirit. (Interestingly, in recent times judō has doubled back toward the secular sphere as it has entered the international arena of competitive sports. How well it maintains its character as a way remains to be seen.) Chicago Bulls coach Phil Jackson's book, *Sacred Hoops: Spiritual Lessons of a Hardwood Warrior*, is a personal account of the author's attempt to cultivate a spiritual life in the turbulent world of professional basketball, something he has had to do without the benefit of the kind of cultural traditions that supported Oh. It is not surprising, then, that Jackson should be more successful at describing the application of meditative principles and practices than he is at revealing the means by which sport itself functions to deepen the inner life. He writes convincingly of how, building on a practice that integrates elements from Zen, American Indian, and Christian traditions, he has used sport as a vehicle for cultivating his own spirituality. But transmitting this sensibility to his players is another matter entirely. However deeply Jackson has been affected by the teachings and techniques he imparts, his players seem to receive them merely as strategies (albeit unconventional ones) for improving their game. For the players, these are simply the elements of Jackson's idiosyncratic coaching style. Nevertheless, Jackson's own experience, like that of Oh, demonstrates the permeability of the boundary between the secret life as it is revealed through sport and through a way.

What is true here for individuals is true for cultures as well. The categories of experience we in the West take for granted are not shared by all cultures, nor is our habit of establishing categories so definitively. In primal societies especially, the lines that distinguish the various realms of experience are both fewer and far more permeable than in our own. As we have already seen, this applies directly to the meaning sport carries and to its relationship to other modes of religious experience.

Highly instructive in this regard is Peter Nabokov's *Indian Running*, an exploration of ancient Native American running traditions. Drawing on his own observations and on the wealth of accumulated ethnological documentation, Nabokov describes traditions of athletic endeavor in which remarkable feats were, and in some cases still are, commonplace: messengers who routinely covered one to two hundred miles a day, ceremonial marathons of more than forty miles, kick-ball races lasting more than two days. Religious ceremony was generally an integral part of Indian running events, for they were rooted in the spiritual sensibility of their societies.

> Indian runners relied on powers beyond their own abilities to help them run for war, hunting, and sport. To dodge, maintain long distances, spurt for shorter ones, to breathe correctly and transcend oneself called for a relationship with strengths and skills which were the property of animals, trails, stars and elements. Without their tutelage and beneficence one's potential could never be realized.

As this passage says, these running events were, like sports in modern Western culture, pursued for a variety of reasons. But, Nabokov tells us, these traditions give vivid expression to something that Western sports culture has largely lost sight of: the innate human hunger for transcendence, for participation in what Eliade calls "the cosmic totality."

Sounding a resonant theme, in *The Marathon Monks of Mount Hiei* John Stevens quotes a statement that informs the monks' singularly severe practice of the buddha way: "If mind and body are unified, there is nothing that cannot be accomplished. Strive to attain the ultimate, and the universe will someday be yours."

And they should know. These monks, select members of Japan's Tendai school of Buddhism, pursue a regimen of religious training that defies generally accepted beliefs about the limits of physical endurance. Though their number is small (as of the book's publication in 1988, there had been only forty-six full-fledged marathon monks in the previous hundred years), their activities have been thoroughly documented on film and in eyewitness accounts, including those of attending physicians.

To become a marathon monk, one must complete a twelve-year period of strict monastic retreat on the sacred Mount Hiei, just outside Kyoto. At the center of the monks' practice is *sennichi kaihōgyō*, the thousand-day mountain marathon. The monk practicing *kaihōgyō* rises at midnight, after three or four hours of sleep. Following a light breakfast, he sets out alone on one of two courses—one close to nineteen miles, the other around twenty-five. With only light straw sandals for foot support, the monk jogs across the mountain's steep and rugged terrain, making frequent stops of several seconds to several minutes, during which he stands, chants, and offers prayers at the more than two hundred shrines and temples along the way.

Completion of the course takes between six and eight hours. But this is not a race, and speed means nothing. What matters is the quality of the monk's consciousness and his strict adherence to the rules—such as no stopping for rest or refreshment, no deviation from the course, and no special accommodation for the mountain's frequently inclement weather. Upon his return, the remainder of the monk's day is taken up with religious functions, chores, two simple meals, and some time for personal care. After lunch, the monk is permitted one hour's rest.

During the first seven years of retreat, a monk will do ten one-hundred-day periods of daily runs. In the sixth year the daily distance covered increases to thirty-eight miles, and in the seventh year to fifty-two.

To accomplish such feats of endurance, the monks learn to practice and rely on deep, controlled breathing, proper rhythm, and intense meditative concentration. And though they rarely discuss it, as practice deepens they find that they tap into a source of power beyond the self that helps carry them along.

But the single most gruelling test of a monk's endurance entails no running at all. It is, rather, a seven-and-a-half-day period of fasting and prayer called *dōiri*. The monk begins *dōiri* on the seven-hundredth day of marathon training, and for its duration he goes entirely without food, water, rest, or sleep. His entire time is spent chanting scripture, performing rituals, and sitting in meditation silently reciting a specific mantra. Although many might argue that such a feat is impossible, witnesses report that the monks emerge from the ordeal looking physically weak but radiant in spirit. Within a relatively short time—as little as two weeks—even the monk's physical strength is restored.

As the monk advances in practice, feelings of hardship decrease, and he finds himself suffused with energy and sustained by joy. Stevens writes:

> At the end, the marathon monk has become one with the mountain, flying along a path that is free of obstruction. The joy of practice has been discovered and all things are made new each day. . . . Awakened to the Supreme, one marathon monk described his atti-

tude thus: "Gratitude for the teachings of the enlightened ones, gratitude for the wonders of nature, gratitude for the charity of human beings, gratitude for the opportunity to practice"—gratitude, not asceticism, is the principle of the 1,000-day *kaihōgyō*.

Whatever one makes of the extreme severity of the monks' training (and I must say that I'm not at all sure what to make of it myself), there is no gainsaying the extraordinary nature of what they do.

Stevens sometimes speaks of the marathon monks as athletes, but I doubt they see themselves that way. (Although, interestingly, their counsel is frequently sought by Japan's professional baseball players.) But whatever the case, other than its physicality, their training doesn't seem to be an athletic undertaking. Marathon monks concern themselves not with the achievement of excellence in performance but with the transformation of consciousness. They do not compete, nor do they play. Most importantly, they pursue their discipline in a realm of the spirit that is quite apart from that borderline realm between jest and earnest that is the true home of athletic play.

Nevertheless, a certain resonance exists between the experience of the marathon monk and that of the athlete. Each in his own way demonstrates that, as Michael Murphy argues, the body possesses extraordinary capacities, which are unleashed when mind and body are unified through dedicated practice. For monk and athlete alike, the rigorous pursuit of a discipline is a response to a prompting within the heart to deepen and intensify experience, and in so doing, to sense in one's being an underlying wholeness.

The Paradox of Selfhood

"Happiness is absorption." Thus wrote T. E. Lawrence, and the statement's truth applies not only to the athlete and the mystic, but to the artist, the farmer, the tax attorney, and the auto mechanic as well. In these moments when the world is experienced, as Zen Master Dōgen writes, with the whole of one's body and mind, the senses are joined, the self is opened, and life discloses an intrinsic richness and joy in being.

In *Anna Karenina*, Tolstoy tells of such an experience with such color and detail that one feels its living quality as though from the inside. Oppressed by worry, the ruminative Levin, whose spiritual struggles are counterposed to the moral and romantic ones of Anna, decides one day to work in the fields alongside the peasants, a highly unusual thing for a landowner to do, even one as eccentric as Levin. Unaccustomed to such rigorous physical labor, he at first fears he will not last even the morning. But as the hours pass, Levin falls into a rhythm that washes away extraneous thoughts and brings his senses to life.

> The grass cut with a juicy sound and fell in high, fragrant rows. On the short rows the mowers bunched together, their tin dippers rattling, their scythes ringing when they touched, the whetstones whistling upon the blades, and their good-humored voices resounding as they urged each other on.

In time he so loses himself in the work that it discloses to him a state of blessedness.

> The longer Levin mowed, the oftener he experienced those moments of oblivion when it was not his arms which swung the scythe but the scythe seemed to mow of itself, a body full of life and consciousness of its own, and as though by magic, without a thought being given to it, the work did itself regularly and carefully. These were the most blessed moments.

Mihaly Csikszentmihalyi describes this as the *merging of action and awareness*. In *The Evolving Self* he writes: "One becomes so concentrated and involved that the usual dualism between actor and action disappears; one does what needs to be done spontaneously, without conscious effort. This unified consciousness is perhaps the most telling aspect of the flow experience."

Concentration on a task frees up psychic energy that would otherwise be focused on the self and its myriad concerns. This focus on the present brings a feeling of enjoyment and a more vital relationship to the world. Csikszentmihalyi quotes a number of sources describing the experience. Some of these accounts are dramatic, such as that of a music composer: "You are in an ecstatic state to such a point that you feel as though you almost don't exist. I have experienced this time and time again. My hand seems devoid of myself, and I have nothing to do with what is happening. I just sit there watching it in a state of awe and wonderment. And [the music] just flows out by itself." Other accounts are more down to earth and are, in their ordinariness, all the more noteworthy. For example, a mother describes the flow she enjoys while spending time with her young daughter. "Her reading is the one thing that she's really into, and we read together. She reads to me, and I read to her, and that's a time when I sort of lose touch with the rest of the world, I'm totally absorbed in what I'm doing."

The range in the depth and intensity of the experiences described is revealing in itself. Whether the experience is a simple moment of peaceful clarity or an epiphany that rattles one to the core of one's being, the principle is the same. When we operate in an integral fashion—with the whole body and the whole mind—we cease to be aware of the sense of self. And greater freedom from the self means greater freedom *for* the self.

Negotiating this paradox of selfhood is a defining feature of the secret life in all its forms. The point yields itself to an endless play of expression. The less self-conscious we are, the more conscious we become. The less self-centered we are, the more centered we become. In the words of the great medieval Christian mystic Meister Eckhart: "The truth is that the more ourselves we are, the less self is in us." And, of course, a salient characteristic of Zen is the particular attention it gives to laying bare, and playing upon, the nature of this paradox. The examples to be found in Zen discourse are countless, but a personal favorite is a phrase I heard many years ago from one master who, in referring to enlightenment, spoke of "realizing the self of no-self."

Sometime in the mid-1970s I read an interview with the basketball star Julius Erving, who was then at the pinnacle of his great career. The interviewer was particularly interested in those occasions when "the Doctor" would so raise his level of play that he seemed to take over a game single-handedly. The key to it, said Erving, was concentration, and the intensity of concentration necessary to play at that level was extremely difficult to maintain. There was nothing particularly new in this, but I was struck by what he said next. The greatest obstacle to sustaining that peak of concentration was not, in Erving's view, failure to make a play—indeed, that might even sharpen one's focus. What was most difficult was to sustain one's focus after a great play, because there was then a strong temptation to dwell on what one had just done. Patting himself on the back robs a player of his composure and diverts his attention from involvement in the action to commentary about the action. The seductive power of pride and elation is extremely difficult to overcome.

The problem Erving described is instantly recognizable to anyone who has pursued a meditative path, the relative newcomer and, I imagine, even the marathon monk. Different though their disciplines may be, athletes and meditators alike must dedicate themselves to a process of training, carried out under special conditions, in which they can, for a time, turn away from the multitude of demands that lay claim to one's attention in daily life and give themselves over to their pursuit. To move ahead, they must be able to find within themselves a delicately balanced sense of confidence that can withstand the doubts and fears that deplete the self yet not be taken in by the sort of pride that inflates the self. Athletes and meditators alike must submit themselves to the confines of their

discipline and, paradoxically, in doing so they find an inward freedom. Within the limits of their activity, the athlete and the student
of the way take measure of the self and in that process they confront the same conundrum—that is, to achieve the objective, one
must get oneself out of one's own way.

I am reminded of a story from some years back that became a
favorite in Buddhist teaching circles. An old man with a long white
beard was asked one day whether he slept with the beard outside or
inside the covers. The man replied that, though he had had the
beard for many years, he had never given the matter any thought,
and so could not answer the question. He promised his interlocu-
tor that he would look into the matter that very night and have an
answer in the morning. When he lay down for bed, the old man first
tried putting his beard outside the covers. But it somehow didn't
feel right, and after a few minutes he switched its position to inside
the covers. But soon that didn't feel right either. So back to the outside, but the result was the same. So he tried inside again. Thus he
spent the entire night: outside, inside; inside, outside—with neither
ever feeling right. The next morning, after having gotten not a wink
of sleep, he still could not answer the question.

The story illustrates the kind of problem that ensues when
consciousness turns back on itself. When the door of self-consciousness is opened, the self becomes vulnerable to all manner of
mental mischief. This is particularly disruptive, even debilitating,
when the self chases its own tail, so to speak, in a downward spiral
of fear, self-doubt, and self-criticism. This dynamic is an essential
feature in most neuroses. The agoraphobic panics over going out in
public because he fears that going out in public will cause him to
panic. The singer is overcome by anxiety about going onstage
because she fears that going onstage will cause her to be overcome
by anxiety.

Most often, the vicious cycle begins with a single trauma. One
day the writer can't find the right words. After a few anxious, doubt-
filled trips around the (mental) block, a simple snag has escalated

into a complete paralysis of ability. Whether it is crippling or relatively mild, the cycle of self-consciousness depletes one's inner reserves of knowledge, intuition, imagination, and mental energy.

To be an athlete is to wrestle with this demon again and again—in the batter's box, at the foul line, on the putting green. Often the demon wins, as when an athlete "chokes" under pressure. Occasionally its victory is so total that it can impede, even destroy, an entire career. Baseball players seem to be particularly vulnerable to this affliction, perhaps because the game's pace allows time for the cycle of anxiety to accelerate and accumulate greater pressure. The more a player dwells upon a problem he is having, the worse the problem becomes. At a certain point, the player feels he has "gone haywire." When that happens, a fine pitcher finds his pitches sailing into the on-deck circle, or a catcher must walk to the pitcher's mound and hand the ball back because his return throws are flying off into center field. The problem is not a loss of skill, and more likely than not, approaching it as such will just make things worse by turning up the pressure.

The situation is enough to drive one to drink, and for athletes, artists, and anyone who must perform on demand, it often does just that. Freud referred to alcohol as a kind of universal solvent for the anxious ego. By dulling consciousness, alcohol, like similar drugs, cuts through the pressure that builds when the self gets embroiled in its own running commentary about itself. Former All-Star first baseman Keith Hernandez said:

> I decided to take a page from my Dad's book. He doesn't drink, but he recommends a one-night binge to break a disastrous slump. He would do it in his own playing days. The idea is to get so wasted you can't get tied up rehashing past mistakes, and you wake up with a clean slate—in a stupor, granted, but with a clean slate.

It was not for nothing that Freud called the ego "the seat of anxiety." Neurotic symptoms, in their extremity, simply make the fundamental situation more clear. Saddled with the responsibility of mediating conflicting demands, controlling impulses, withstanding the superego's perfectionist recriminations, and negotiating the endless travails on the path of life, the Freudian ego is a tragic figure. Caught between a rock and a hard place, the ego, like any conscious organism, seeks to maintain and enhance its existence, yet that very existence is a burden from which it craves relief.

It is true that in sport, as in any realm of life, the vicissitudes of the self can be augmented by the pressure to perform. But going more directly to the heart of the matter is another truth: the essence of our love of sport is the deliverance it brings from the burdens of selfhood. The freedom that sport bestows comes not through the dulling of consciousness but through its refinement, not through dissolving the ego but through transcending it. It is hardly a rarity for athletes to be self-absorbed egotists. But in those moments in which the whole of their being is absorbed in the pursuit of excellence, the self is put aside and deep reserves of mental and physical power become available. At its best, sport shows us that the egoic self is only a small part of who we are and that to live entirely within its familiar parameters is to experience only a small part of the life we are given.

But excellence does not come without its risks. Sports psychology confirms through science something that athletes learn through experience: to perform well one must maintain a positive frame of mind. Confidence is critical, even when it is thoroughly unrealistic. One must learn to produce positive thoughts on demand, and should negative thoughts arise, as they surely must, one must learn to push them out of consciousness.

As Norman Vincent Peale insisted a half century ago, positive thinking is indeed powerful. But as his predecessors Freud and Jung knew, a sunny outlook can cast a long shadow. The basic rule of the unconscious is that that which is repressed will, in time, be expressed. When unwanted aspects of the personality are shunted aside, they return unbidden, now hostile and distorted. The chaotic, mean, and selfish lives led by so many athletes is the price paid for the one-sided development of the personality to which, through the single-mindedness of their focus, they become susceptible.

Our fears, doubts, flaws, and weaknesses are essential aspects of our humanity. To deny these traits is to deny who we are and, even worse, to deny what we can become. Our greatest growth comes in facing them. In accepting them, our lives are enriched by the healthy expression of the energies they hold. Those traits that we would most like to be rid of are, most often, the very traits we most need if we are to feel in daily life a sense of fullness, to find in our being a durable measure of completeness.

Should-be Hall of Famer Pete Rose once said, "I'd walk through hell in a gasoline suit to play baseball." The statement, like his play, demonstrates a marvelous love of the game. But there is something awry in the ferocity of the sentiment. Rose's well-known problems off the field were, I think, a distorted reflection of his virtues on the field. Like many an athlete, the game gave him a means to give luminous expression to the intensity of his spirit. But life outside the game provided his energies no such creative channel, and he never developed the inner skills to cultivate satisfying new ones.

We love sports for the relief they bring from the burdens of selfhood. In that, they are a source of enrichment. But for the very same reason they can be a kind of addiction. Referring to a fan as a "sports junkie" is usually a well-meant exaggeration of a benign passion. But when that passion mutates into obsession, then sport ceases to be part of a life well lived and becomes the cause of a neglected life lived partially.

For Plato, sport was the "twin sister" of the arts for the cultivation of the soul and the harmonizing of body and mind. Sport is abundant in the virtues it displays and powerful in its capacity to awaken those virtues in the soul, either through play or contemplation. Sport brings essential nourishment to the inner life, and we should ask no less of it. But the virtues of sport are not without limit, and we should not ask too much of it.

Sport is not the whole of life, but it ushers us into life's wholeness. Sport may not make one a better person, but by showing much of what is best in us, it can help. It may not bring spiritual enlightenment, but it does display the spirit's dazzling glow. Sport rarely brings substantive self-knowledge, but few things so readily connect us with the source of self-knowledge: the center of our being, the self of no-self, that place within the swirl of action where we find what Rilke called a "stillness like the heart of a rose."

CHAPTER FIVE

Between Art and War

> If you could bottle all the emotion let loose in a basketball
> game, you'd have enough hate to fight a war and enough
> joy to prevent one.
>
> BILL RUSSELL

In the opening sequence of Martin Scorcese's film *Raging Bull*,
as the credits roll, the slow-motion camera remains fixed on the
solitary figure of Robert DeNiro, as Jake LaMotta, performing the
ritualistic warm-up drills of the boxer's craft. Bobbing, tucking,
moving inside to work the body of his imagined foe, then pacing his
corner like a caged panther, the violence of the fighter's movement
is accompanied by the heartbreaking loveliness of the strains of
Pietro Mascagni's opera *Cavalleria Rusticana*. The total effect is
mesmerizing—an atavistic rite graced with balletic refinement. It is
perhaps the most inspired moment in what is certainly among the
finest of all films dealing with sport.

The harshness of the black-and-white photography and the
compressed fury of DeNiro/LaMotta's movements convey a sense
of what Aristotle referred to as sport's "brutal element." Yet set in

slow motion against the music's poignancy, the fighter's menacing dance appears, at the same time, as a revelation of balance, agility, grace, and strength. In this single scene, Scorcese captures the essential polarity of beauty and violence from which sport emerges.

The fighter's hooded robe hides his face—the most visible expression of one's individuality. LaMotta's individuality is indeed expressed here, but only insofar as it is a unique incarnation of the form of his sport.

Generally, sports movies are stories about an athlete's personal life, and this one will be, too. In fact, the very next scene shows LaMotta in retirement—a washed-up, overweight palooka, as pathetic outside the ring as he was awesome within it. In cutting from the opening sequence to this first scene, a polarity of another sort is revealed—that which obtains between, on the one hand, the personal experience of the individual who attains excellence as an athlete and, on the other, the transpersonal activity of those natural forces of which the athlete is the embodiment. The life of an athlete who has given himself over to a sport is not entirely his own. It belongs, in part, to the designs and culture of the sport he pursues.

I've heard it said that contradiction is the logic of the human soul. It may also be said, I think, that contradiction is the logic of the soul of sport. In these opening sequences, Scorsese highlights and makes explicit contradictions that are fundamental to the athletic experience. The poles of aesthetics and brutality, as well as those of the personal and impersonal claims upon the self, are linked together in a living relationship and thus made to work upon the viewer. The film provides no real answers to the conflicts it illustrates. These tensions are creative, giving rise to a moment of consciousness broad enough to contain them, and their resolution lies in their depth and complexity.

Films like *Raging Bull*, Ron Shelton's *Cobb*, and John Sayle's *Eight Men Out* portray the athlete's moral universe as being far more complex and conflictual than the one that was depicted in the sports films on which I grew up. *Pride of the Yankees, Knute Rockne,*

All American (which featured Ronald Reagan as Notre Dame's George Gip), *The Babe Ruth Story* (in which William Bendix, as the Babe, not only hits home runs for kids in hospitals but even manages to save the life of a dog that somehow wanders into the outfield and gets struck by a line drive)—these and other such films made the lives of sports figures into sentimental morality plays. Evoking Hollywood's vision of Main Street, USA, they tell of solid churchgoing families, hardworking moms and pops, wise-cracking but good-hearted teammates, crusty but good-hearted coaches, and neighborly, patriotic communities undivided by racial and class antagonisms. (Is it any coincidence that years later this same untroubled fantasy of American society was the mythic cornerstone of Reagan's "Morning in America" presidency? The Gipper managed to evoke nostalgia for a past that had existed only in the movies.)

Fundamental to these movies was the idea that the morality of the world of sport and the morality of the social sphere are coextensive. On the field, the virtues athletes exhibited were the same that off the field made for good citizens. Sports build character, as the saying goes. Or at least went. Nowadays, the idea that the virtues of sport translate readily to the rest of life is difficult to take seriously. This is not just a matter of cynicism; it is a matter of facing reality. As with celebrities from other fields, the private lives of our star athletes have assumed a public nature. We simply know too much about them. In a passage from his *San Francisco Chronicle* column, Scott Ostler gives humorous expression to current public perception of the character issue:

> Baseball gave us the hotfoot, the bubble-gum-and-tobacco wad, throwing firecrackers at babies, and the time-honored tradition of sitting naked on a teammate's birthday cake.
>
> With Darryl Strawberry, though, we just might be looking at the possibility that some guys simply are not mature enough to be baseball players.

The turn toward a more realistic attitude about sport's morality is for the best, I think. Certainly it has made for better art. The best of recent sports films are not only better than those I saw as a child, they are excellent cinema in their own right. By delving into some of the sports world's darkest personalities and events, they bring to light vital truths, truths that cannot be reconciled with the vision of sport promulgated by those wishing to impose upon it a conventional moral agenda.

In certain respects, greater public realism has also enriched the culture of the sports world, though the loss of illusion has come at a considerable price. Our skepticism has led us to confuse the meaning of sport with the corrupt business of sport, to view sport's proper moral limits as indicators of its moral bankruptcy, and to assume that the existence of false values means the absence of real ones.

Shadow Play

Heraclitus wrote, "Strife is the source and the master of all things." Nowhere is the power of this idea more apparent than in sport, in the *agon*. Conflict is the form of sport and the source of its profound virtues. But the conflict in sport is present not only in the competition between opponents. Sport also displays the conflicts in the human heart.

Jung saw the tension between opposing aspects of our nature as the creative basis of psychological life. But when only one side of a polarity is allowed to function, the psyche becomes unbalanced, stunted, or disruptive. Sport draws upon not only the socially sanctioned and personally acceptable aspects of human nature but on their opposites, their shadow side, as well. By making us intimate with our inner contradictions, sport carries us into the fullness of our being.

In a letter to a friend, Nietzsche told of an experience that came over him as he stood at a hill's summit just as a storm erupted.

> The storm broke with tremendous force, gusting and hailing, and I had an indescribable sense of well-being and zest, and realized that we actually understand nature only when we must fly to her to escape our cares and afflictions. . . . Lightning and tempests are different worlds, free powers, without morality. Pure will, without the confusions of intellect—how happy, how free!

Like a tempest, an athletic event is a "different world," a world of natural powers unhindered by the normal constraints of society's moral conventions. This is not to say that sport's second world is without morality—far from it. The rules, structure, means, and aim of sport establish a well-defined moral context, but it is a context that is distinct and is subject to the sport's own designs. The morality of sport requires that the powers of body and soul be unleashed—sometimes to the extent that they threaten to erupt into chaos—but once manifest, these powers are contained, channeled, and integrated into the coherent pattern of athletic craftsmanship.

In the arena and on film, Jake LaMotta and Ty Cobb each embodied sport's brutal element. Both were violent men in whom the love of conflict burned fiercely. In their extremity, they gave clear demonstrations of one of sport's great mysteries: the inward act by which the heart's dark passions can, through discipline and dedication, be harnessed for the achievement of excellence, beauty, and perhaps even a measure of personal redemption. The best of virtues abide in the worst of us, and the worst of vices live in the best of us. Our fascination with sport derives in part from its capacity to embrace and make noble the truth that good and bad are inextricably bound together in our lives and in our hearts.

Hemingway once called Cobb "the greatest of all ballplayers—and an absolute shit." Juggle the wording of the first clause and the sentiment can apply to LaMotta and countless other athletes (and artists too, not least among whom, many say, is Hemingway himself). *Raging Bull* and *Cobb* do not ask that we admire their protagonists. Nor do they ask that we feel sympathy. What they do ask is that we appreciate the awesome task of wringing greatness from the darkness of the soul. In their unsparing depiction of the emptiness and cruelty of the lives of Cobb and LaMotta, the films also startle us into recognition of the ruinous effects these powers, once awakened, can visit upon those whose mastery of them is limited to the confines of a particular discipline.

The Art So Long to Learn

In *Second Wind* Bill Russell addresses the beauty and the brawl of athletics by observing that all sports are "a mixture of art and war." How the two mix varies from sport to sport and from player to player. In every sport, writes Russell, there is a proper balance between the two factors, a balance that is maintained through the rules of play. By modifying the rules by which a sport is governed, its mixture of art and war can be readjusted. But this is not something to be done lightly. With too much tampering, the balance of contrasting elements, which is essential to a sport's unique character, is destroyed. Although his subject was not sport, Heraclitus's observation that "harmony is the result of a tension between contraries, like that of the bow and the lyre," has an uncanny resonance with Russell's point.

Russell notes the tremendous commercial pressures in big-time athletics to broaden a sport's appeal by altering the balance in favor of the pole of war. Enjoyment of a sport's artistry requires sophistication on the part of the spectator. One need not be well versed in the fine points of strategy and execution to be drawn into the heat of the struggle for victory. It does not take a connoisseur to appreciate displays of raw power: the knockout punch, the crunching tackle, the in-your-face slam dunk. But to those whose knowledge does not embrace the game's complexity and nuances, much of its beauty remains hidden. As I wrote in the introduction, like literature, music, drama, or any other art, a sport reserves its deepest rewards for those who regard it with a cultivated and loving appreciation.

In his book *Magic's Touch*, Magic Johnson (who is one of the very few, perhaps the only player to equal Russell's mastery of the team game) writes, "To *really* watch a game you have to think like a player." Thinking like a player—that is, an intelligent player—is a considerable task. Call to mind, if you will, the image of Magic leading his Laker teammates of old on a fast break. The play's success depends on his ability, and that of his teammates, to weigh accurately the merits of dozens of variables—to recognize options, assess likely outcomes, evaluate the capabilities of each teammate and opponent, recall how the players involved responded in similar situations, read how the patterns of the play are likely to unfold, discern the emotional climate on the court and in the stands, note the dictates of the overall flow of the game—this, and more, must all be done in the space of two or three seconds.

Among hoops fans, Magic's long dedication to refining his physical skills is well known. But, as he recounts, he began at an early age to develop a complementary basketball intelligence. While still a youngster, he studied the game under his father's tutelage, learning to see the whole floor, to understand the elements that make for a successful play, to recognize situations early on and anticipate how they would develop. Russell, too, writes of his long hours of rigorous mental training: visualizing plays, studying his opponents, searching out fine details of basketball strategy, learning to read the intricacies of the game's many facets. Like physical skill, athletic intelligence is most effective when it functions intuitively. All athletes, when they are at their best, sense that they can act without thinking. But the best athletes also think without thinking—that is, their thinking flows freely, unencumbered by self-consciousness or deliberation.

Basketball (and baseball, football, tennis, and so forth) may be "just a game." But to be played right, it requires of its practitioners the application of great intelligence. David Miller writes that play is "characterized not by lack of seriousness but by lack of correspondence to external reality." The same can be said of most art. Athletes like Bill Russell and Magic Johnson take their art very seriously.

But even to use the phrase "just a game" betrays a kind of fragmentary thinking, a utilitarian logic that ignores the irreducible value of the game's activity, of the play. As the Romantic philosophers argued, the experience of freedom and coherence, which is paradigmatically conferred by play, is essential to a meaningful life. One of Romanticism's most prominent figures, J. C. F. Schiller, wrote that "man plays only when he is in the full sense of the word a man, and he is only wholly a man when he is playing." As I discussed in chapter 3, Romanticism found in the creativity of play—in the beauty, order, emotion, imagination, and liberty of spirit it expresses—is the basis for an aesthetics of art and, more importantly, for the art of living.

Whether or not one subscribes to the Romantic view, the connection between sport and art is insistent. Russell notes that the connection is evident in the way we talk about sport. We speak of the beauty of an exceptional play or the artistry of a great player. And we mean it. The words are true to the exhilaration and wonder we experience.

Years earlier, Johan Huizinga noticed much the same thing. In *Homo Ludens*, he wrote:

> The words we use to denote the elements of play belong for the most part to aesthetics, terms with which we try to describe the effects of beauty: tension, poise, balance, contrast, variation, solution, resolution, etc. Play casts a spell over us; it is "enchanting," "captivating." It is invested with the noblest qualities we are capable of perceiving in things: rhythm and harmony.

Sport and art are also linked by the similar moral ground they each occupy. Each is in its own right an ethical imperative, in need of no justification because it is good in itself. Each is a distinct realm of experience, with its own moral dictates and moral limits. In *Testaments Betrayed* Milan Kundera observes that a novel is "a realm where moral judgment is suspended." He writes: "Suspending moral judgment is not the immorality of the novel. It is its morality. The morality that stands against the ineradicable human habit of judging instantly, ceaselessly, and everyone; of judging before, and in the absence of, understanding."

In discussing aesthetic experience, James Joyce sounded a resonant theme. The radiance of the aesthetic experience moves one simply to behold the object—not possess it, reject it, or criticize it. One is absorbed by the work's rhythms and harmonies, by the movement of its elements and their relationships to each other and to the work as a whole.

In sport and art both, the suspension of conventional moral thinking is essential if they are to draw freely upon the full range of human experience. Through discipline, training, and mastery, practitioners of each transform the lead of life's raw ingredients into gold—that is, into a *work* that feeds the soul and liberates the spirit. The imposition of an extrinsic moral agenda can only undermine this alchemy.

This is not to say that artists or athletes are above the moral claims of the social world. Although all too many seem to think they in fact are, this is a personal failure of the practitioner, not of the practice. As Aristotle said, wisdom demands that we distinguish among life's various contexts and act in a manner proper to each.

But sport, like art, is too compelling to exist in isolation. It is too rich in what we might call *action parables* to be mute about moral life. Sport can—indeed, it should—help teach us to become better persons. But it teaches best when it does not try to teach at all—that is, when it teaches not through moral injunction but through the virtues it embodies and the experiences it elicits. Sport accomplishes its task of moral instruction not by imparting flimsy bromides but by stimulating a sensibility that seeks to discern the complex patterns in the workings of human virtue.

George Will's *Men at Work* is a gem of sports literature. One of the things that makes it so is its lack of moral preachments. Will is, of course, best known as a conservative political commentator. Like anyone in his line of work, moral questions are essential to his concerns. Like many a conservative, he is especially at home when he is decrying what he perceives as the moral failings of others. But in exploring the world of baseball, he wisely follows Aristotle's advice and checks his moral baggage at the door. By doing so, he brings the moral center of baseball, and of sport in general, into sharp focus. The key is right there in the book's subtitle: *The Craft of Baseball*.

Clearly, writing the book was a labor of love—and appropriately so. Will knows that the love of a sport is a gift, for sports are generous in the satisfactions they provide. But to thrive, a sport must make demands in return. It must be approached as a craft, as something requiring one's respect, appreciation, and care.

In *The Parliament of Fowls* Geoffrey Chaucer wrote, "The lyfe so short, the crafte so long to learne." Some six hundred years later, Chaucer's words find an echo in an oft-quoted remark by Ted Williams on his own craft of baseball: "Don't you know how hard this all is?"

Williams's statement, unlike Chaucer's, is not expressive of particular eloquence or insight. What makes it notable is the great force it carries and great authority with which it rings. Williams knows, as few people ever have, just *how* hard baseball really is. He knows how long it takes to learn to play the game with excellence, and he knows how long it takes to learn that there is no end to the learning. In other words, he knows baseball as only a master can know his craft.

For John Updike, Williams was the epitome of the athlete who always cares about himself and his craft. This care is the essential and priceless moral lesson of sportscraft. By investing an activity with one's dedication, aspiration, discipline, skill, and knowledge, one's identity is linked to it. In some indefinable way, part of one's self is in the work. Through craftsmanship, a sport becomes an expression of the athlete's total self and the means by which the self recognizes its own excellence. Excellence, *arete*, is not just the aim of the athlete's striving; it is also the moral basis of that striving, for in excellence is found freedom. A sport is a structure in which the truth of this is lived out and imprinted on the soul. For this reason, a sport is, like any craft, an object worthy of care.

In his concluding pages, Will discusses another Ron Shelton baseball film, *Bull Durham*. *Bull Durham* is not dark and troubling the way *Cobb* is. To the contrary, it is filled with affection and good cheer. But it is equally unsentimental, and as he does in *Cobb*, in *Bull Durham* Shelton relishes the chance to overturn the clichés of the sports-film genre. There are no great victories, no lessons in fair play or sportsmanship, and—blessedly—no role models. But there is a hero of sorts: the journeyman catcher "Crash" Davis. Crash embodies the film's moral theme, as well as that of Will's book.

Crash has labored anonymously at the game for twelve minor-league seasons. Will writes of him: "In terms of physical skills, Crash is not much. But in terms of character, he is the real keeper of the flame of craftsmanship." Against his wishes, Crash is saddled with the task of teaching the lessons of sportscraft to "Nuke" LaLoosh, a young pitcher who is as rich in talent as he is poor in the understanding of how to use it and of what it means to use it well. Crash rides Nuke mercilessly, and when Nuke asks why, Crash responds: "'Cause you don't respect yourself, which is your problem, but you don't respect the game—and that's my problem." Morally speaking, this is, as Will observes, the heart of the matter.

Respect for the game is not something one learns all at once and forever. Throughout his college career, Bill Bradley was the personification of basketball craftsmanship. But in confronting the painful difficulties of adapting to the pro game, he found a deeper level of appreciation for the "integrity and completeness of the game in itself." As he told the *New Yorker* writer Michael Kelly:

> After that first year with the Knicks, with the way the public, the audience, treated me, I always had a great deal of ambivalence, and therefore I never gave myself to the public. And as a result, you know, I came to feel that it was my performance on the court and the integrity of what we were doing there in and of itself that mattered, and that the millions watching were incidental to what the craft was—and that realization was a liberation.

For Bill Russell, respect for the integrity of the game contributed to his decision to retire. In *Second Wind* he tells of an incident from his final season as a player—a season in which he was the Celtics' head coach as well—that confirmed his intention to bring his playing career to a close at season's end. In the final seconds of a tied game against the Baltimore Bullets, the Celtics stole the ball and called time out. With the crowd in a frenzy and his players, pumped with adrenaline, huddled around him awaiting instructions, Russell broke out in laughter—and not just a chuckle, but great, rolling cascades of laughter. Seeing the confusion in the players' faces, he calmed himself and tried to explain the humor of the situation.

> I said, "Hey, this is really something. Here I am a grown man, thirty-five years old, running around semi-nude in front of thousands of people in Baltimore, playing a game and yelling about killing people. How's that?" I looked at my teammates as if I'd really said something profound, and they looked blankly as if I hadn't said anything.

The incident erased any doubts he still may have harbored

about retiring: "In all my years of laughs in pro basketball, I had never mocked the game itself. You can't give out what a game requires if you start focusing on its ridiculous aspects."

Noble Struggle

The element of artistry in sport must, as Russell says, be balanced by the element of warfare. Recall that the Greek term *agon* could denote either an athletic contest or a military conflict. The formal quality of conflict and struggle—whether its display is primarily physical, as in boxing, or mental, as in chess—is essential to sport and is the source of much of its pleasure. It is reasonable that, for many a thoughtful person, this should be troubling. It certainly seems to have been so for the ever-pensive Aristotle. But although he was critical of the "brutal element" in sport, the philosopher was nonetheless in awe of Olympic champions. Indeed, he even tried his hand at sportswriting of a sort, having worked on a list recording Olympic victories down through the centuries.

Obviously, there is good reason for our discomfort with sports violence. Less obviously, there is wisdom to be found in that discomfort, for it is, in part, discomfort with ourselves, with what James Hillman calls "the martial state of the soul."

A Zen saying has it that "not knowing is the most intimate"— that is, our deepest and fullest experience of self and world is revealed when we cease to impose upon phenomena the conceptual mind's habitual categories of thought and perception and see the world with fresh eyes. However distinctively this notion might be applied in the context of Zen training, in matters of inward understanding, I find it works as a general principle. For example, in finding the wisdom of our unease with sports violence, a little less certainty and a bit more openness than is generally evident in discussions of the subject would be well in order. Too often, the issue is clouded over with stale arguments and preconceptions. To seek justification for categorically accepting or rejecting sports violence is to seek a simplicity that is misleading. Violence in sport is not wholly good nor is it entirely bad. It is, however, complex.

The connection between sport and war extends back deep into humankind's history. As William Baker observes, the earliest competitive games took their form from the hunting and warring activities of primitive peoples. Competitions in running, fighting, swimming, jumping, throwing spears and stones, shooting arrows—all these were tests of an individual's abilities as a hunter and warrior. The equipment used in modern sport—balls, bats, sticks, rackets, to say nothing of such items as javelins and épées—derive from the stones, clubs, knives, spears, and such that were, for our ancient forebears, implements of survival.

However aggressive they may have been (and they were often aggressive to an extreme), ritualized competitions were a method of settling questions of status and honor that was far less lethal than actual combat. Though the patterns of social behavior and organization in contemporary societies differs in many ways from those of primitive ones, sport remains tied to such matters. Baker writes: "Tribal honor as well as material benefit fell to the strongest, fastest, most efficient hunters. . . . For the successful modern athlete who wins social status and personal esteem on the one hand, material reward on the other, only the form—not the essence—of the primitive competitive impulse has changed."

Just as the language of sport links it to art, so does its language link sport to war. Examples are countless. Two power forwards fight for position under the boards. A tennis player battles back to win the match. A quarterback leads his team into the opposition's territory. A batter guards the plate; a goalie guards the net. A team attacks the weak points in the opposition's defense. Even Kareem Abdul-Jabbar's sky-hook—as perfect and consistent an expression of physical grace, rhythm, and harmony as one is likely ever to see—was generally noted not for its aesthetic grandeur but for its effectiveness as an "offensive weapon."

In his famous essay "The Moral Equivalent of War," William James wrote, "So long as antimilitarists propose no substitute for war's disciplinary function, no *moral equivalent* of war, analogous, as one might say to the mechanical equivalent of heat, so long they fail to realize the full inwardness of the situation." In James's view, the creation of such an alternative to war was the most important task of his time. Clearly, the need is no less urgent today. Ever since the essay's publication a century ago, some have argued that an alternative—namely, sport—already exists. That sport might fit the bill is hugely, and naively, optimistic. Practically speaking, organized games have been around nearly as long as organized warfare, and the evidence that they have done much to relieve us of the horrors of war is pretty thin. Indeed, sport seems every bit as popular in the most warfaring of societies as it is in more peaceful ones. But in another way—one more modest but still of great importance—sport does speak to the urgency of James's concerns. Sport will never replace war, but it can and does help us to "realize the full inwardness of the situation."

For those who seek justification, of whatever measure, for the violence in sport, understanding the inwardness of war generally means first acknowledging that aggression is an innate feature of human nature. We are, they say, warlike in our very constitution. Starting from this premise, some approximation of Freudian drive/discharge theory provides a logical basis for viewing sports violence as justified, even healthy. The instinctual energy of aggression must in some manner be discharged. Lest we all go about murdering one another, societies must find minimally destructive means by which this energy can be vented. Seen in this light, sport is cathartic. Sports purge violence from our breasts by channeling aggressive energy into activities that contain and make virtue of it.

Then there is the coin's other side. Arguments against the violence in sport have it that violence begets further violence. Aggressive behavior is reinforced by activities in which it is condoned. From this perspective, sport's aggression may serve the function of allowing us to let off steam, but the benefits of this venting are short-lived. In the larger picture, the effect of the violence in sport is to promote, rather than discourage, further violent behavior, both within athletic confines and beyond them.

Both arguments make sense, and each can be persuasive. Notwithstanding their contradictory status, each perspective carries a measure of truth. But both are marred by the same flaw: each approaches the problem with a moral, rather than an experiential, attitude. Such an approach is simply not adequate to matters of inwardness, which call not for conceptual closure but for open exploration. We would do better simply to acknowledge that in certain situations—sport and combat among them—violence has its own attraction, which, to be understood, must be attended to.

In *A Blue Flame* James Hillman begins his discussion of war by recalling a scene from the 1970 film *Patton,* in which the famous general walks the field of the previous night's intensely fought battle. As he surveys the carnage, he stops by a dying American officer. The general picks up the soldier, kisses him, and looking out upon the wreckage, says, "I love it. God help me, I do love it so. I love it more than my life."

For Hillman, as for James, those who seek peace must account for and respect war in all its inwardness. The love of battle voiced by Patton exerts a strong pull on the soul, and to ignore or deny this can only undermine whatever peaceful intentions we may have. Hillman argues that "to know war we must enter its love," for "it is a principle of psychological method that any phenomenon to be understood must be empathetically imagined."

Traditionally, a culture's religious mythology has provided symbolic forms by which its members could honor warfare's hold on the psyche. In the Greek pantheon, the war god Ares occupied a place of prominence, as did Mars, his counterpart in Roman mythology. In Norse and Germanic mythology, Odin was the "All-Father," chief among gods and the patron of warriors, seers, and poets. The war god Ogún of West African and Afro-Caribbean mythology was, and in places still is, honored for his creative as well as his destructive power. Ogún is associated with the element iron and thus with the implements—for farming, hunting, building, and fighting—essential for civilization, both in war and peace.

Hillman points out that great battles constitute the setting and much of the content of the epic tales that are the religious basis for cultures throughout the world: the Babylonian Gilgamesh, the *Iliad* of Greece, the *Aenead* of Rome, the Hindu *Mahābhārata* (which includes the *Bhagavad Gita*) and *Rāmāyana*, the Norse *Eddas*. The Bible is replete with tales of battles fought on Yahweh's behalf, culminating with the apocalyptic vision of Revelations.

These mythic figures and religious texts do not shrink from war. Their stories tell of a world in which powerful forces collide, in which human purpose is clarified in defending the forces of life (represented by a bounded group, such as the tribe or nation) against the powers of destruction and chaos as represented by a threatening Other. Read psychologically, the religious mythology of warfare tells us that the martial spirit— whether personified by war gods and heroes or given narrative shape through legend and lore— holds a prominent place in the psyche and is essential to its completeness. Read as metaphor, mythic warfare speaks of our deepest struggles of the spirit, of tests of our character, of our resolve to lay claim to the longed for peace, wisdom, or redemption we seek.

War has rightfully been called the summary of all evils. We moderns have been fortunate in that methods of historical and social analysis have, to a degree, chastened us in our romance with war. We are, it seems, no less violent than people of earlier times, but there is something to be said for the fact that today there is little room for argument with the blunt assessment of Air Force General Curtis LeMay: "I'll tell you what war is about. You've got to kill people, and when you've killed enough they stop fighting." True to his word, LeMay killed unapologetically, indiscriminately, and often.

But while war may be the summary of evils, evil is not the

summary of war. "Cry 'Havoc!' and let slip the dogs of war," declaims the vengeful Marc Antony in Shakespeare's *Julius Caesar*. War embodies all that is worst in human experience, yet confronting its cruel havoc demands of the warrior much that is most noble: self-sacrifice, courage, honor, loyalty, camaraderie. Indeed, it was not uncommon among ancient and traditional peoples—for example, the Celts and many Native American societies—to regard the display of strength, bravery, and skill to be warfare's primary objective, viewing conquest as a matter of secondary import.

According to Rick Fields, author of *The Code of the Warrior*, the figure of the warrior, as both a source of misery and an expression of nobility, occupies an uneasy position in both society and the psyche. Fields focuses his study on societies with developed cultic martial traditions, such as that of the Plains Indians of North America, the samurai of Japan, and the knights of medieval Europe. In such societies, warriors were seen to serve a religious function as protectors of life. In the proper fulfillment of their role, they were honored for embodying the most esteemed virtues of the spirit. But a society had also to protect itself from the "sins of the warrior," from transgressions against the very people warriors are sworn to protect. Because of this destructive potential, a warrior, to be honorable, had to live by a strict code, which constrained and channeled the power with which he or she was entrusted.

Powerful energies are at work in the martial life. Our word *berserk* derives form the Old Norse *berserkir*, "those wearing bearskins," the name given to the devoted warriors of Odin. In preparation for battle, berserkirs sang and danced and shouted wildly, working themselves into a "holy rage," and then rode into battle abandoned to this ecstatic state. In his study of the myths of Northern Europe, *The Well of Remembrance*, Ralph Metzner writes that controlling and directing the intense energy of the battle fury was a serious matter. To illustrate, he cites the Celtic legend of Cuchulain, who became "so overheated with battle rage that a group of naked women was sent out to confront him and bring him out of his rage-trance. Even so, he had to be lifted into vats of cold water, which he caused to boil and evaporate."

Such mythic hyperbole may mislead us into thinking that the intoxicating fury is more foreign than in fact it is. To contain and manage the power of the warrior cult, to protect itself against martial transgression, a society must impose upon its warring class a strict code of discipline to which that class is bound by both law and honor. Parallel to this, the martial energies of the psyche require management and constraint. "Whether invited or not, the gods will be present." Mars, in particular, does not take kindly to being ignored. He erupts destructively from his repressed confines, invading and distorting our thoughts and acts. The energies that find personification in the god of war have a rightful and necessary place within the psyche. From these martial powers come vigor, drive, and primal joy in the decisive acts and blazing exultations of the body.

Ted Williams said, "There's only one way to become a hitter. Go up to the plate and get mad. Get mad at yourself and mad at the pitcher." Some might argue that Williams's advice does not work for everyone, but no one who knows baseball would suggest that it did not work for Williams himself. Williams was as good a hitter as the game has seen. His observation and his success illustrate Hillman's claim that sport is a means of refining our angry and aggressive impulses, of making them instruments of purpose rather than expressions of random emotion:

> As the amatory arts improve the skills of desire, so sports improve the skills of anger. The coach, for instance, before each game speaks the rhetoric of Mars and unleashes a raging exhortation to impassion his team with the spirit of fight. So, too, the glaring stare of the boxer. A player in every opponent sport must learn, first of all, the skills of anger: how to let it rise, contain it, not "lose" it or "choke." Also, how skillfully to provoke the anger of the opponent so that he or she makes errors and commits fouls. Even

solo sports . . . require the skillful management of anger where the explosive charge upon which successful action depends never crosses over into blind attack.

Mars, or Ares, is not, of course, the only god at work in sport, and his warring spirit is not the only psychic state that sport must honor. For example, it was Hermes, the messenger of the gods and "the companion of men," who in his unrivaled generosity toward humankind brought to us boxing and gymnastics. Hermes is a complex, "mercurial" figure, comprising many qualities. Among his many roles, Hermes was the discoverer of fire, protector of travelers and domestic animals, guide to the dead, and master artisan. But he was also a "trickster," a god of thievery and deception. Just as sport honors Ares through the refinement of anger, so does it honor the cunning and inventiveness of Hermes. As in trickster tales throughout world mythology, in sport the morality of trust and good faith is turned on its head. Deception is of the highest virtue, integral to the athlete's artistry. Hermes' cunning finds expression in head fakes, crossover dribbles, no-look passes, stolen bases, curveballs, and countless other forms of trickery.

Sport also honors the martial goddess Athena, protectress of cities and staunch adversary of Ares. Whereas Ares is known for his bursts of red-faced fury, Athena's most characteristic attributes are intelligence and skill. As both warrior and patroness of craftspersons, she might be said to bridge the realms of art and war. Her inspiration is evident in practical inventiveness, technical skill, self-mastery, confidence and serenity amid travail, and intelligent discernment. As both friend and guide, she figures prominently in the tales of Heracles, Odysseus, and Achilles—the preeminent models for Western civilization's classical conception of heroism.

The Right Stuff

It is in the figure of the hero that the inward mythic link between sport and war finds its fullest expression. Indeed, even in our age of postmodern irony, stories of heroic figures and deeds retain an essential place in our talk of battle, whether martial or athletic, for in battle an individual's reality is reduced to the perfect clarity of a single, luminous encounter.

But the connection between athletic and martial heroism is not purely psychological. In much of the ancient world, great tribal chieftains, valiant warriors, and legendary heroes were honored and celebrated in athletic contests. We know that as early as 1800 B.C.E., Celtic tribes in Ireland regularly held competitive games in honor of departed heroes, and it is probably safe to assume that similar events occurred elsewhere in pagan Europe. Egyptian competitions were conducted in homage to the great deeds of pharaohs. Both the *Iliad* and the *Odyssey* contain descriptions of funeral games honoring fallen warriors that predate the first recorded Olympic games, held in 776 B.C.E., by several centuries.

The main figure honored by the Olympics was Zeus, first among the gods. But winners of the competitions were celebrated in their own right. Poets sang their praises, athletes offered prayers before statues of great champions of the past, and upon their return home, victors were greeted with great celebrations and showered with gifts, for the entire citizenry, and the spirit of the city itself, shared in the glory won on the playing field.

Today, heroes stand on shaky pedestals, which are eroded by irony, proximity, and confusion. The great epics of antiquity were set in what Eliade calls the "age of the heroes," a distant, mythologized past. The historical events on which the *Iliad* and *Odyssey* are based occurred about four centuries before Homer. Though the actual causes of the Trojan War were probably no less sordid than those of most wars, by the eighth century B.C.E., when Homer gathered and shaped the fragments of legend into poetic narratives, the events had already been mythically transformed through generations of oral transmission. The great battles recounted by Homer were fought in concert with the workings and wishes of the gods, not simply to protect Exxon's profits or further the nation's geopolitical strategic objectives.

The saying that no man is a hero to his valet has gained a new level of significance in a time when communications technology and the cult of celebrity have made us all valets of a sort. We are too close to our heroes. We see their dirty laundry, and we're disappointed, yet strangely gratified, to find it is no different from our own. More significantly, in knowing them up close and personal, we trespass an essential boundary. Heroes need distance—if not in time and place, than at least in the imagination. We perceive heroism not in the details of someone's personal life but in the actions of those who embody something beyond the personal. Not personal traits but transpersonal powers are what identify the hero.

We are leery, as we should be, of the image-making machinery that converts heroism into a commodity. The heroic aura depletes itself when its considerable power is put to work selling Wheaties or Reeboks. We would feel very differently about Achilles, and Homer as well, if the *Iliad's* description of Achilles famous shield told us that it carried the Hellenic equivalent of a corporate logo.

But irony and cynicism are not the main factors assailing our sensibilities about the hero. The main problem is that we've got the whole matter mixed up. In the classical Western conception, heroism is demonstrated through noble struggle. Exemplary moral conduct is, well, exemplary, but it is not necessarily heroic. Nor is it a virtue a hero must possess.

Today we have conflated the function of the hero with those of the role model and the celebrity. The hero, in whom the qualities of noble activity constellate, is someone to honor, not to emulate. Great athletes deserve our respect and appreciation, but few are worthy of emulation. Good role models for the young are, and have always been, essential to society. But the stadium or the arena is a place for watching heroes. A good English teacher is a far better role model than a basketball star cum Nike pitchman.

Several months prior to this writing Mickey Mantle died. Though cancer was the proximate cause of death, it was well known that Mantle's years of hard drinking had taken their heavy toll. Coverage in the press seemed to focus more on Mantle's alcoholism than on the very thing that made his death newsworthy in the first place: his greatness as a baseball player. In delivering the eulogy, the sports broadcaster Bob Costas spoke of Mantle as "a fragile hero to whom we had an emotional attachment so strong and lasting that it defied logic."

But all heroes are fragile in some way. As F. Scott Fitzgerald wrote, "Show me a hero and I will write you a tragedy." Still, the vulnerability of Achilles' heel did not diminish his heroism, and neither should Mantle's own Achilles heel compromise his. Costas gets to the heart of the matter when he speaks of Mantle's capacity to inspire an attachment that defies logic. This is what heroes do. The figure of the hero resonates in a layer of the psyche much deeper than reason.

The great poets of ancient Greece composed odes in praise of the magnificence of athletic heroism. The poet best known for this was Pindar of Thebes, who wrote:

> For if any man delights in expense and toil
> and sets in action high gifts shaped by the gods,
> And with him his destiny
> Plants the glory which he desires,
> Already he casts his anchor on the furthest edge of bliss,
> and the gods honor him.

Heroes represent something bigger than themselves. Their acts carry magical, or archetypal, meaning. Their struggles are tests of fate. Their victories bestow blessings upon the populace. In surmounting the obstacles before them, they symbolically share with all the divine energy, the Right Stuff, that they embody.

Sports heroes may think that they act on their own behalf, but that is true in only a narrow sense. They are like the single-combat warriors of ancient times; their triumphs symbolize the victory of the powers of beneficence. Jung observed that artists are rarely able to grasp and assimilate the deep psychic forces their work expresses. The same is true of athletes. The deepest meaning of an athlete's greatness belongs not to the athlete but to the sport. Whether consciously recognized or not, that meaning is felt in the most inward recesses of all who share in loving the game.

In June 1995, while in the midst of researching this book, I traveled to New York for a family gathering. Just before I left for New York, a friend put me in touch with Pat Toomay, the former defensive lineman with the Dallas Cowboys and Oakland Raiders. At the time, Pat was living in upper Westchester County, just a twenty-minute drive from where I would be staying at the home of my brother and his family.

Several days after my arrival, Pat and I got together at the small cottage he was then renting. With the sounds of Sonny Rollins and Miles Davis playing softly in the background, we passed the day absorbed in conversation about sport, spirituality, and the meeting of the two.

At the time, Pat was hard at work on a book of his own, his fourth. His workspace reminded me of my own: books piled everywhere, notes to himself taped to any remaining surface space, a meditation cushion in the corner. Even many of the authors we were consulting were the same: Eliade, Jung, Huston Smith, and the like.

Our meandering conversation would return consistently to several themes, most prominently the heroic role of the athlete. Pat spoke frequently, and with some bitterness, of the ways high-level athletes are pressured to deny their deepest sense of themselves in order to maintain an acceptable public image. The culture of big-time sports actively discourages self-reflection, and this for two reasons. The first and most obvious is to enforce conformity to institutional norms. But the deeper reason is that "those who take on the role of hero pay a deep price, and our culture doesn't recognize that, and we'd rather that our athletes didn't either. Our stance toward our heroes is out of touch with reality."

Pat points out that for the Greeks, "heroes were capable of every sort of abomination—incest, murder, rape, you name it." Today, we scramble to cover up the darkness of the hero archetype, and in so doing we have split its organic fullness. Unable to accept our heroes' contradictions, we regard them with resentment and contempt when their imperfections cause us discomfort.

Abruptly, Pat turns and begins lifting up stacks of books and rifling through notes as he searches for something. Finally, he's got it: volume 1 of Eliade's *History of Religious Ideas*. He flips through the pages until he finds the right passage, then hands it to me. Eliade writes that those who attain excellence run the risk of "arousing inordinate pride and insolence (*hybris*)" for which the gods impose as punishment *ate*, temporary madness. "This is as much as to say the *hybris* and its result, *ate*, are the means that in certain cases (heroes, kings, adventures, etc.) bring about the realization of *moira*, the portion of life allotted at birth to such mortals, whether they are overambitious or are simply mislead by the idea of excellence."

According to Pat, "high-level athletes live in a bubble, in many ways cut off from other people and from themselves." Ego inflation may feel great, but it can make chaos of one's life and relationships. There is probably nothing like being the object of the adoration of thousands or millions, but when it goes to one's head, pain is sure to follow. Besides, being an object of adoration is, after all, being an *object*. One can easily lose any real sense of being a subject, of being oneself. Even the hero who remains level-headed must surrender something of his or her personhood in sacrifice to the honor of the role, and personhood is a difficult thing to recover.

At the end of our meeting, as I drove back to my brother's, my thoughts turned to Muhammed Ali, for me the epitome of the athletic hero. In Ali the contradictions, the virtues and flaws, of the heroic character were made vivid. In his days as an athlete, Ali was a man of both joyous and deeply troubling passions. In his training camp he would take time out to perform magic tricks for children and carry on to the delight of everyone. But he could also be cruel. Outside the ring, he shamelessly and unfairly taunted Joe Frazier, calling him stupid, a gorilla, an Uncle Tom. In the ring, in a state of battle frenzy, he sadistically tormented the overmatched Floyd Patterson and Ernie Terrell for refusing to call him by his Muslim name.

But to my mind, no one in my lifetime has so embodied athletic virtue. His blend of physical gifts, of grace, speed, and strength, was a wonder to behold. More importantly, the skill and intelligence with which he put these gifts to use was unmatched. But he had something else, something more. José Torres, a world champion himself, writes of Ali's ability to call up "those mysterious forces." Call it heart, intensity of spirit, the Right Stuff. I think of it as mana.

The "Thrilla in Manilla" was perhaps the single most extraordinary sporting event in modern times. Ali and Frazier, rivals for the ages, linked by destiny, pushing each other deeper and deeper into the purity of their passion.

But for me, the most memorable single moment in Ali's career occurred in his first fight with Frazier, in 1971. Talk about single combat! Ali was coming back to regain the title that had been taken from him for refusing to be drafted for Vietnam. The fight reflected the split in the country. For millions who opposed the war, Ali was our champion. Those who supported the war, or felt it wrong to protest, or just hated Ali, threw their support behind the apolitical Frazier. It did not take long to see that Ali's four-year banishment had taken its toll on his abilities. He fought a great fight, but Frazier clearly had the upper hand. In the final round, with Ali visibly exhausted and hurting, Frazier struck him square on the chin with a staggering left hook. Calling Ali "the most valiant fighter I've ever seen," the referee, Arthur Mercante, would later say, "Frazier hit him as hard as a man can be hit. . . . [Ali] went down, and anyone else would have stayed on the canvas." But Ali got right up, taking the mandatory eight-count while standing. At the time, listening on the radio. I didn't take note of the extraordinary thing that had just happened. I couldn't see the punch, and besides, I was too distraught about Ali's losing the fight. But in the intervening years, whenever I see that moment on film, I am left speechless by the display of a spirit that was simply unconquerable.

Today Ali is a hero to most every sports lover, even those who used to hate him. Partly, it is because the passage of time and being out of the spotlight has created more of the distance of heroism. Partly, it is because of his charm. But it is also because he has paid a price for his heroism, and he has done so without regret. His excellence led him to *hybris*, but despite his physical afflictions, his spirit seems now to be at peace with his *moira*, with his portion of mortal life. Ali will always be The Greatest. But today he shows us not only his greatness but also a remarkable degree of goodness.

Many say that we need heroes to show us how great we can be. I disagree. Heroes do something much more rare and important. They show us how great they are, and in so doing, they allow us to participate in that greatness. I am not speaking of living through them vicariously, though that does occur. What I mean is that through them we live mythically. Through the mana they gather and bestow, they help us to feel the gem-like flame of life's majesty. For this they deserve our discerning yet unreserved gratitude.

Acknowledgments

To name all those who directly or indirectly had a hand in the completion of this book would require another volume. While my gratitude and appreciation go out to them all, some deserve special mention.

In our interviews David Meggyesy, Tom Singer, Michael Murphy, and Pat Toomay gave freely from their wealth of insight and experience. Beyond that, for each this generosity of spirit extended to include the sharing of resources, suggestions for additional avenues of research, writerly knowledge and information, and friendship.

Scott Ostler, Barbara Gates, Wes Nisker, Melvin McLeod, Rick Fields, Debra Horowitz, Spencer Koffman, Beatrice Motamedi, Michael Katz, Michael Wenger, Gordon Nicholson, Christopher Bamford, and Steve Weintraub read all or part of the manuscript at various stages. Their criticism and encouragement contributed much to the book and to its author.

To Leslie Daniels; Chuck Davis; Donald Rothberg; Patrick McMahon; Carla Javits and Margaret Cecchetti and their kids,

Tony and Sonya; Michael Flanagin; Susan, Dale, Luke, and Emily Bowyer; Lynn Kameny; Elihu Smith; Mudita Nisker; Dan Clurman; Marcia Freedman; Jack Scott; John Gasparoni; Gene Vlansky; and Steven Goodman—many thanks for the many ways you've all helped. Special thanks go to Anita Feder-Chernila, stalwart friend and guide through thickets and thorns, and to my oldest friend in the world, Steven Schlussel, and his daughters, Elizabeth and Lucinda.

I am grateful to Samuel Bercholz and the staff at Shambhala Publications, especially the crew of editors who worked on this book: Peter Turner, Emily Hilburn Sell, Larry Hamberlin, and Kendra Crossen Burroughs.

Carl and Sue Prince, in-laws *extraordinaire*, were kind and patient in propping up my often sagging self-confidence. An author and historian, Carl's many suggestions were an especially big help in the manuscript's early stages.

My brothers John and Dan have throughout their lives shared with me the love of athletics. Since the book's inception they have freely given their help in whatever ways they could. Through them and their wives, Rosa and Wendy, my life has been graced by four glorious nieces and one equally glorious nephew. Samantha, Tanya, Kimmy, Allie, and Dylan consistently give me new reasons to believe in the essential goodness of sport and of life.

My parents, Nathan and Caryl, deserve my deepest gratitude. From the beginning, they have taught me about the love of sports and the love of ideas. And they have done it most lovingly.

It has been my great good fortune to have had many beneficent teachers and mentors in the secret life, and to them all I am forever grateful. But in writing this book, I have felt with special keenness the influence of one: the late Taizan Maezumi Roshi. Every day gives me new cause to appreciate his limitless life.

Finally, there is the home team. Without the insistence, persistence, assistance, and existence of my wife, Liz, there would be no book at all. Our daughter, Alana, thoughtfully waited until right after the completion of the manuscript's first draft to make her entrance onto the stage of this life. Since the moment she was born, she has revealed effortlessly the workings of the *lumina natura* in the events of daily life. They are my greatest blessing.

Bibliography

Aitken, Robert. *The Mind of Clover: Essays in Zen Buddhist Ethics.* San Francisco: North Point Press, 1984.

Angell, Roger. *Season Ticket: A Baseball Companion.* Boston: Houghton Mifflin, 1988.

Baker, William J. *Sports in the Western World.* Totowa, N.J.: Rowman and Littlefield, 1982.

Brasch, R. *How Did Sports Begin? A Look at the Origins of Man at Play.* New York: David McKay Company, 1970.

Campbell, Joseph. *The Masks of God: Primitive Mythology.* New York: Viking, 1959.

———, with Bill Moyers. *The Power of Myth.* New York: Doubleday, 1988.

Csikszentmihalyi, Mihalyi. *Flow: The Psychology of Optimal Experience.* New York: Harper & Row, 1990.

———. *The Evolving Self: A Psychology for the Third Milennium.* New York: HarperCollins, 1993.

De Rougemont, Denis. *Love in the Western World.* New York: Pantheon Books, 1956.

Deshimaru, Taisen. *The Zen Way to the Martial Arts.* New York: E. P. Dutton, 1982.

Dryden, Ken. *The Game: A Thoughtful and Provocative Look at a Life in Hockey.* New York: Times Books, 1983.

Eagleton, Terry. *Literary Theory.* Minneapolis: University of Minnesota Press, 1983.

Edinger, Edward F. "The Tragic Hero: The Image of Individuation." *Parabola*, I, no. 1, 1975: 66–73.

Eliade, Mircea. *A History of Religious Ideas: From the Stone Age to the Eleusinian Mysteries.* Chicago: The University of Chicago Press, 1978.

Eliot, T. S. *Collected Poems, 1909–1962.* New York: Harcourt, 1963.

Fields, Rick. *The Code of the Warrior.* New York: HarperCollins, 1991.

Fischer-Schreiber, Ingrid, Franz-Karl Ehrhard, and Michael S. Diener. *The Shambhala Dictionary of Buddhism and Zen.* Boston: Shambhala Publications, 1991.

Fitzgerald, F. Scott. *The Great Gatsby.* New York: Scribner, 1925.

Flavell, Linda and Roger. *Dictionary of Word Origins.* London: Kyle Cathie Limited, 1996.

Frankfort, H. and H. A., John A. Wilson, and Thorkild Jacobsen. *Before Philosophy: The Intellectual Adventure of Ancient Man.* Chicago: University of Chicago Press, 1946.

Freud, Sigmund. *A General Selection from the Works of Sigmund Freud.* Edited by J. Rickman. Garden City, New York: Doubleday Anchor, 1957.

Gadamer, H. G. *Truth and Method.* New York: Crossroad, 1984.

Gallwey, Timothy W. *The Inner Game of Tennis.* New York: Random House, 1974.

Gasperoni, John. "The Experience of Self-Doubt: A Phenomenological Investigation." Ph.D. diss. California Institute of Integral Studies, 1985.

Giamatti, A. Bartlett. *Take Time for Paradise: Americans and Their Games.* New York: Crossroad, 1984.

Gould, Stephen Jay. *Dinosaur in a Haystack: Reflections in Natural History.* New York: Harmony Books, 1995.

Harrison, Jane Ellen. *Themis: A Study of the Social Origins of Greek Religion*. New Hyde Park, N.Y.: University Books, 1962.

Hauser, Thomas. *Muhammad Ali: His Life and Times*. New York: Simon & Schuster, 1991.

Hemingway, Ernest. *The Old Man and the Sea*. New York: Charles Scribner's Sons, 1952.

Hillman, James. *Re-Visioning Psychology*. New York: Harper & Row, 1975.

———. *A Blue Fire: Selected Writings by James Hillman*. Edited by Thomas Moore. New York: Harper & Row, 1989.

Huizinga, Johan. *Homo Ludens: A Study of the Play Element in Culture*. Boston: Beacon, 1950.

Jackson, Phil, and Hugh Delehanty. *Sacred Hoops: Spiritual Lessons of a Hardwood Warrior*. New York: Hyperion, 1995.

Jackson, Susan Amanda. "Elite Athletes in Flow: The Psychology of Optimal Sport Experience." Ph.D. diss., University of North Carolina at Greensboro, 1992.

Jacobi, Jolande. *The Psychology of C. G. Jung: An Introduction with Illustrations*. New Haven: Yale University Press, 1973.

James, William. *The Varieties of Religious Experience*. New York: Random House, 1902.

Johnson, Earvin "Magic" Jr., and Roy S. Johnson. *Magic's Touch*. Reading, Mass.: Addison-Wesley Publishing Company, 1989.

Jung, C. G. *Modern Man in Search of a Soul*. New York: Harcourt Brace, 1936.

———. *Memories, Dreams, Reflections*. New York: Random House, 1961.

———. *Man and His Symbols*. New York: Dell, 1968.

Kerrane, Kevin and Richard Grossinger, eds. *Baseball I Gave You All the Best Years of My Life*. Oakland: North Atlantic Books, 1977.

King, Billie Jean, with Kim Chapin. *Billie Jean*. New York: Harper & Row, 1974.

Kundera, Milan. *Testaments Betrayed*. New York: HarperCollins, 1995.

Leonard, George. *The Ultimate Athlete: Re-Visioning Sports, Physical Education, and the Body*. New York: Avon Books, 1977.

Lowry, Dave. *Sword and Brush: The Spirit of the Martial Arts*. Boston: Shambhala Publications, 1995.

Maezumi, Hakuyu Taizan. *The Way of Everyday Life*. Los Angeles: Center Publications, 1978.

Maslow, Abraham. *The Farther Reaches of Human Nature*. New York: Penguin, 1971.

McPhee, John. *A Sense of Where You Are: A Profile of Bill Bradley at Princeton*. New York: Farrar, Straus and Giroux, 1965.

Meggyesy, Dave. *Out of Their League*. Berkeley: Ramparts Press, 1970.

Metzner, Ralph. *The Well of Remembrance: Rediscovering the Earth Wisdom Myths of Northern Europe*. Boston: Shambhala Publications, 1994.

Miller, David. *Gods and Games: Toward a Theology of Play*. New York: World, 1970.

Murphy, Michael. *Golf in the Kingdom*. New York: Delta, 1972.

———. *The Future of the Body*. Los Angeles: Tarcher, 1992.

———, and Rhea A. White. *The Psychic Side of Sports*. Reading, Mass.: Addison-Wesley Publishing, 1978.

Nabokov, Peter. *Indian Running*. Santa Barbara: Capra, 1981.

Naiman, Arthur. *Every Goy's Guide to Common Jewish Expressions*. New York: Ballantine Books, 1981.

Nietzsche, Friedrich. *The Gay Science*. Translated by Walter Kaufmann. New York: Vintage Books, 1974.

Novak, Michael. *The Joy of Sports: End Zones, Bases, Baskets, Balls, and the Consecration of the American Spirit*. New York: Basic Books, 1976.

Oh, Sadaharu, and David Falkner. *Sadaharu Oh: A Zen Way of Baseball*. New York: Times Books, 1984.

Okrent, Daniel and Steve Wulf. *Baseball Anecdotes*. New York: Oxford University Press, 1989.

Pelé, with Robert L. Fish. *My Life and the Beautiful Game: The Autobiography of Pelé.* Garden City, N.Y.: Doubleday, 1977.

Plaut, David, ed. *Speaking of Baseball: Quotes and Notes on the National Pastime.* Philadelphia: Running Press, 1993.

Ravizza, K. "Qualities of the Peak Experience in Sport." In *Psychological Foundations of Sport,* edited by J. M. Silva and R. S. Weinberg. Champaign, Ill.: Human Kinetics, 1984: 452–462.

Ricoeur, Paul. "The Model of the Text: Meaningful Action Considered as a Text." *Social Research,* 38, 1972: 529–562.

Ridge, Julie, and Judith Zimmer. *Take It to the Limit.* New York: Rawson Associates, 1986.

Rilke, Rainer Maria. *Duino Elegies.* Translated by. J. B. Leishman and S. Spender. New York: W. W. Norton, 1939.

Roberts, Michael. *Fans! How We Go Crazy Over Sports.* Washington, D.C.: The New Republic Book Company, 1976.

Russell, Bill, and Taylor Branch. *Second Wind: The Memoirs of an Opinionated Man.* New York: Random House, 1979.

Schwartz, Tony. *What Really Matters: Searching for Wisdom in America.* New York: Bantam Books, 1995.

Scott, Jack. Bill Walton: *On the Road with the Portland Trail Blazers.* New York: Crowell, 1978.

Singer, Thomas, and Stuart Copans. *A Fan's Guide to Baseball Fever: The Official Medical Reference.* Mill Valley, California: Elijim Publication, 1991.

Stein, Murray, and John Hollwitz, eds. *Psyche and Sports.* Wilmette, Ill.: Chiron Publications, 1994.

Stevens, John. *The Marathon Monks of Mount Hiei.* Boston: Shambhala Publications, 1988.

Stump, Al. *Cobb: A Biography.* Chapel Hill: Algonquin Books, 1994.

Syer, John, and Christopher Connolly. *Sporting Body Sporting Mind: An Athlete's Guide to Mental Training.* Cambridge, England: Cambridge University Press, 1984.

Thompson, Robert Farris. *Flash of the Spirit: African and Afro-American Art and Philosophy*. New York: Vintage Books, 1984.

Tolstoy, L. N. *Anna Karenin*. Translated by Rosemary Edmonds. New York: Penguin Books, 1978.

Toomay, Pat. *The Crunch*. New York: W.W. Norton, 1975.

Umminger, Walter. *Supermen Heroes and Gods: The Story of Sport through the Ages*. New York: McGraw Hill, 1964.

Weiss, Paul. *Sport: A Philosophic Inquiry*. Carbondale and Edwardsville: Southern Illinois University Press, 1969.

Will, George. *Men at Work: The Craft of Baseball*. New York: HarperPerennial, 1991.

Wilson, Colin. *The Essential Colin Wilson*. Berkeley: Celestial Arts, 1986.

Wolfe, Tom. *The Right Stuff*. New York: Farrar, Straus, Giroux, 1979.

Yogananda, Paramhansa. *Autobiography of a Yogi*. New York: The Philosophical Library, 1946.